52

"teacher"

THE HENRIETTA MEARS STORY

Marcus Brotherton

Regal

From Gospel Light
Ventura, California, U.S.A.

PUBLISHED BY REGAL BOOKS
FROM GOSPEL LIGHT
VENTURA, CALIFORNIA, U.S.A.
PRINTED IN THE U.S.A.

Regal Books is a ministry of Gospel Light, a Christian publisher dedicated to serving the local church. We believe God's vision for Gospel Light is to provide church leaders with biblical, user-friendly materials that will help them evangelize, disciple and minister to children, youth and families.

It is our prayer that this Regal book will help you discover biblical truth for your own life and help you meet the needs of others. May God richly bless you.

For a free catalog of resources from Regal Books/Gospel Light, please call your Christian supplier or contact us at 1-800-4-GOSPEL *or* www.regalbooks.com.

All Scripture quotations unless otherwise indicated are taken from the *King James Version.* Authorized King James Version.

Other version used
The *New King James Version.* Copyright © 1979, 1980, 1982 by Thomas Nelson, Inc. Used by permission. All rights reserved.

© 2006 Regal Books
All rights reserved.

Library of Congress Cataloging-in-Publication Data
Brotherton, Marcus.
  Teacher / Marcus Brotherton.
    p. cm.
  ISBN 0-8307-3347-7 (trade paper)
  1. Mears, Henrietta C. (Henrietta Cornelia), 1890- 2. Sunday-school teachers—
Biography. 3. Presbyterians—United States—Biography. I. Title.
  BV1518.M4B76 2006
  268.092—dc22
  [B]   2006022633

1   2   3   4   5   6   7   8   9   10   /   10   09   08   07   06

Rights for publishing this book in other languages are contracted by Gospel Light Worldwide, the international nonprofit ministry of Gospel Light. Gospel Light Worldwide also provides publishing and technical assistance to international publishers dedicated to producing Sunday School and Vacation Bible School curricula and books in the languages of the world. For additional information, visit www.gospellightworldwide.org; write to Gospel Light Worldwide, P.O. Box 3875, Ventura, CA 93006; or send an e-mail to info@gospellightworldwide.org.

DEDICATION

William Taber Greig II (1921-2006)
A world Christian and champion of excellence
in Christian education

Chairman of the Board of Gospel Light (1989-2006)
President of Gospel Light (1972-1997)
Vice President of Gospel Light (1950-1972)

Mr. Greig was involved in Christian publishing for more than
55 years. During the late 1950s and early 1960s, he traveled with
Henrietta Mears to her various speaking engagements. It is with
deepest appreciation and love that the people of Gospel Light
remember Mr. Greig for his worldwide vision that carried
the work of Henrietta Mears into the present.

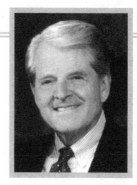

Contents

Acknowledgments

This book is meant to be a readable interpretation of the life of Henrietta Mears, and not an exhaustive research project. In that aim, I am indebted to many authors, educators and researchers who have labored to document and preserve history.

Central to this work are multiple articles and writings of and about Henrietta Mears, including a long-selling book she wrote called *What the Bible Is All About*; a catalog of her citations called *431 Quotes from the Notes of Henrietta C. Mears,* compiled in 1970 by Eleanor Doan; and several transcribed talks, including "The Romance of the Sunday School," "Who Are the Young People You Teach?" "Train Up a Child" and "Dimensions of Leadership."

Central also is a 1966 biography titled *Henrietta Mears and How She Did It* by Ethel May Baldwin and David Benson. Ms. Baldwin was the longtime administrative assistant of Henrietta Mears and also knew her as a friend. The book was researched anew and rewritten in 1990 by Earl Roe, then a senior editor at Regal Books, and published under a new title, *Dream Big.*

Thanks also go to Andrea Madden, who researched Henrietta Mears in an unpublished 1997 master's-level thesis for Gordon-Conwell Theological Seminary. In researching her dissertation, Ms. Madden pored over the extensive primary sources on hand in the archives of Gospel Light, including old church bulletins, flyers, brochures, unpublished Sunday School lessons, tape recordings, journals and letters (she notes that it took about four full days to sift through the material), and also conducted extensive phone interviews with people who knew Henrietta Mears directly, including, Bill and Vonette Bright, Dale Bruner, Louis Evans,

Jr., and Colleen Townsend Evans, Bill Greig Jr., Jack and Anna Kerr, Anne Shelton and Christy Wilson, Jr. Another student, Betsy Cox, wrote a master's thesis in 1961 about Henrietta Mears for Fuller Theological Seminary, which was written while Henrietta Mears was still alive.

Also used as a resource is the work of Dr. Richard Leyda, chairman of the department of Christian Education at Talbot School of Theology, Biola University, who researched extensive primary and secondary source material for Henrietta Mears for a lengthy inclusion in the "Christian Educators of the Twentieth Century" website database project.

I am also indebted to Barbara Hudson Powers for the use of her excellent biography resource *The Henrietta Mears Story,* written in 1957. When she was a young woman, Barbara Hudson (who is still alive and in her 80s today) worked closely with Henrietta Mears for 14 years and was considered by many to be Miss Mears's protégé. To obtain material for her book, Barbara relied on firsthand evidence of her interaction with Henrietta Mears over the years; she also held a series of taped interviews with her. Some of the material for *Dream Big* and *Henrietta Mears and How She Did It* was gleaned from Barbara Hudson's original work. Earl Roe obtained permission to use the material, according to Ms. Hudson Powers, and so have we.

Again, my heartfelt thanks go to all the people who have so diligently researched the life of Henrietta Mears.

I am equally thankful to Deena Davis, managing editor of Regal, for her continued vision and excellent editing skills throughout this project.

An Incredible Lineage

*If we think we are solely responsible for someone's
decision to follow Christ, we forget the history of those
who have labored before us.*

—PASTOR RON KINCAID
SUNSET PRESBYTERIAN CHURCH, PORTLAND, OREGON

After my good friend Paul died of lymphoma at age 36, his
wife found resonance in Don Miller's book *Blue Like Jazz*.
It reminded her strongly of how her husband had thought and
communicated—his life at once splendid and unresolved, like a
passing note of a beautiful chord. Paul was a pastor, a missionary,
a lover of Christ and of creativity, and had lived with a strong desire
to influence the world for God. His widow, through the pages of
Miller's book, was drawn to the heart of Christ, where she found
solace, comfort and support like no other voice could do for her.

The arms, legs, hands and feet of Christ minister to us in
such varied ways—sometimes so silent, so secret is this influence that we hardly notice at first. We may be spurred on or held
in position, reached and comforted, challenged and moved forward. Yet the little-noticed influence is so alive that the world
thunders with its reverberation even after the passage of time.

Consider the lineage of ministry for a moment. What pre-
cedes the thing that touches us and affects us more than we
may appreciate? For instance, how did Don Miller's book find

its way into the hands of Paul's widow?

The first book Miller wrote, *Prayer and the Art of Volkswagen Maintenance*, never topped a best-seller list. Some time later, when Don was known by so many, I met him and told him that I had bought one of his original *Volkswagen* books. He laughed, thanked me, and said, "So, you were 1 of the 15." Miller had considered giving up his writing career after his first publishing dud. But he didn't. He persevered and wrote his second (highly successful) book, *Blue Like Jazz*, which, as not many people are aware, also floundered desperately when it first came out—until Campus Crusade for Christ got hold of it.

For more than half a century, Campus Crusade's unprecedented presence on college campuses has been inseparably linked to its founder, American evangelist Bill Bright. Dr. Bright was in his eighties and battling a degenerative lung disease during the time when Miller's book was read by a Campus Crusade staffer. Yet Bright, and those who carry on his work, possessed the uncompromising vision to reach college students with the gospel.

Already Dr. Bright had championed another young author, Ted Dekker, who went on to write the best-selling Circle trilogy (*Black, Red, White*) and influenced thousands for the sake of Christ. Bill Bright knew the power of words in communicating spiritual truths. Knowing that Don Miller's book would connect well with students, the organization that Bill Bright founded placed an order for 60,000 copies of *Blue Like Jazz* to put in their Freshman Survival Kits. The next year, Campus Crusade ordered 65,000 more—a staggering launch forward for any young writer. Those two huge orders from Campus Crusade arguably solidified Miller's writing career from then on.

So ministry to Paul's widow happened through Don Miller's book because of Campus Crusade for Christ, which was founded by Bill Bright.

Let's back up a step further. What or who were Bill Bright's influencers? What unlikely set of circumstances led someone like Bill Bright to come to a place of ministry in which he could create a tipping point for a writer who would one day minister to a grieving widow in a voice that touched her in a unique way? What a realization—and responsibility—for all of us when we grasp how closely the Body of Christ links and joins us all!

Backtracking the Lineage

Born in Oklahoma in 1921, Bill Bright was reared to be anything but Christian. He described himself as a "happy pagan" in his youth. While in his early twenties, he moved to Los Angeles, California, and founded a fancy-food company called Bright's California Confections. His single-minded drive to make money as a businessman seemed to be set in stone.

But in 1944, while attending Hollywood First Presbyterian Church, Bright turned over the reins of his future to Jesus Christ, and he began a new and earnest road of service for the Lord. There was one problem: Bill's longtime girlfriend and fiancée, Vonette Zachary, wanted nothing to do with Christianity. Vonette described her motivation for moving to California as wanting "to rescue Bill from fanaticism." The two decided to break their engagement when she couldn't dissuade him from following Christ.

Bill and Vonette knew they could never begin a lifelong marriage partnership if they couldn't agree on what had become most important in Bill's life. So Bill made one last desperate plea. He asked Vonette to meet with Teacher, the nickname of the director of Christian education at his church. Teacher was the same extraordinary spiritual leader who had been instrumental in leading Bill to the faith. Vonette agreed to meet, spent 90 minutes talking with Teacher and turned her life over to Christ. Later, a newly married Bill and Vonette moved into this woman's home, where for several years Teacher mentored them in the faith.[1]

During those years under the direct spiritual tutelage of Teacher, Bill and Vonette became infused with a passion to reach college campuses with the message of the gospel of Jesus Christ. The Brights' vision grew clear. Beginning on the campus of UCLA, Bill and Vonette began an outreach ministry, soon naming it Campus Crusade for Christ. Today this ministry has more than 20,000 full-time staff and 663,000 trained volunteers in 181 countries. In addition to its campus ministries, Campus Crusade acts as an umbrella for a variety of far-reaching ministries, including Athletes in Action, Josh McDowell Ministries, Student Venture, the Jesus Film, and more. One report suggests that more than 3.4 billion people have heard the gospel through the ministry begun by Bill and Vonette Bright.

So who was the woman who was so instrumental in the Brights' lives? Who was Teacher?

A Roll-Call Legacy

Teacher was the same woman who helped develop the faith of a mind-boggling list of modern-day Hebrews 11-style Christians.

Consider just one of those names—Billy Graham.

In the late 1940s, when Billy Graham was beginning his ministry, he described himself as a young, skinny, "bag of bones" evangelist. Without the strong backing of a church denomination, as was required in his day, Billy's first evangelistic meetings went all but unnoticed. People considered him a country preacher with an overly simplistic faith and laughed at him for being 50 years out of date. The man who would later become "America's pastor" and "the world's preacher" said of himself in those early years, "I did not feel I had much to say."[2]

Most troubling was Billy's internal conflict over Scripture. He was intrigued by the writings of liberal theologians who rejected its inspiration and authority, which caused Billy to question a core issue on which much of his entire ministry would become based: Could the Bible be trusted completely?

In 1949, just weeks before Billy's Los Angeles crusade, he went to Forest Home conference center in the hills above Los Angeles as a guest speaker. During his time at Forest Home, Billy searched the Scriptures for answers. He prayed. He pondered. After much consultation with Teacher, the same woman who had helped Bill and Vonette Bright, he ended up alone in the woods, on his knees before God. Billy knew that if he could not trust the Bible, then he could not go on. It was there that he made one of the most pivotal decisions of his life. He leaned strongly in the direction presented to him by the woman of faith who had counseled him so well, worked through his doubts and accepted the Bible as God's Word. Period.

When Billy came down the mountain, he was ready to go forward in his calling. The Los Angeles crusade expanded and exploded over an 8-week period, encompassing a record 72 meetings. Billy preached 65 full sermons during those weeks and gave hundreds of additional evangelistic talks to small groups, as well as on the radio. In his autobiography *Just As I Am,* Billy Graham states that as a result of his pivotal time in the mountain woods, he now preached with a new confidence and fervor and no longer struggled internally. He wrote, "There was no gap between what I said and what I knew I believed deep in my soul." Major newspapers, radio stations and magazines such as *Time* and *Life* picked up the story of the Los Angeles crusade's success. Billy would learn during the next few weeks that the phenomenon of the Los Angeles campaign would forever change the face of his ministry.

History knows what happened to Billy Graham in succeeding years. Rev. Graham's worldwide ministry spanned more than five decades and reached literally billions of people. He was pastor and spiritual counselor to a broadly diverse, incredibly far-reaching cadre of influencers, presidents, history makers, celebrities and world leaders, including Harry S. Truman, Winston Churchill, Dr. Martin Luther King, Jr., John F. Kennedy, Indira Gandhi, Queen Elizabeth, the Shah of Iran, Muhammad Ali, Mikhail Gorbachev, Pope John Paul II, Boris Yeltsin, Bill Clinton and George W. Bush.

Yet it all came back to this one spiritual mentor, Teacher, who helped pass on a legacy of faith to Rev. Graham. In a tribute to the woman who counseled him at Forest Home, Billy Graham described her as "one of the greatest Christians I have ever known."

The list continues. This same woman had a similar amazing influence on

- United States Senate Chaplain Richard Halverson
- Author and Bible translator J. B. Phillips
- Cowboy film actors Roy Rogers and Dale Evans
- The Navigators founder Dawson Trotman
- Young Life founder Jim Rayburn
- Seminary president Charles E. Fuller
- A multitude of pastors, Christian authors, college presidents, committed Christian business leaders, church and parachurch leaders, lay pastors and missionaries throughout North America and around the world.

Undoubtedly, this woman has left an unprecedented legacy of spiritual lineage and faith influence that continues today. In addition to the countless leaders she influenced for Christ, the effect of her life can be felt in the organizations she founded: Gospel Light Publishers, Forest Home Christian camping and conference ministries, and GLINT (Gospel Literature International Publishers—whose nonprofit ministry is now fulfilled by GLW (Gospel Light Worldwide), providing rights worldwide for language translation of Regal's books and Gospel Light's Sunday School curriculum.

Teacher was a woman who helped shape her world—and ours. Most likely she has touched your life for the cause of Christ, perhaps in ways you will never know.

Who was this woman? Who was Henrietta Mears? She was not a university professor, a pastor, a president, a celebrity or an American idol.

She was a Sunday School teacher. From that unlikely position, Henrietta Mears became a hero of the faith.

This book is a story of scope and influence, showing how one person helped shape the world. Plenty of people have dreams that never amount to anything, but Henrietta Mears's life story shows that dreams can become reality. At its core, this is a story about the Holy Spirit and how He radically and remarkably moves in people who are completely sold out to the Lord.

As I read through the various accounts of Henrietta Mears's life, I often found myself needing to stop and pray. Her accomplishments made me feel at once overwhelmed, chastened, inspired and motivated. I only hope I can live a life that is a fraction as influential for the cause of Christ as hers.

Miss Mears never married. She passed away in 1963, at age 73, five years before I was born. Had I been given the opportunity to meet with her today, I'm sure she would encourage me in the faith with the same words she spoke to encourage countless others: "Start where you are, as you are, in serving the Lord."[3]

In that same spirit of optimism and passion, I invite you into the presence of Henrietta Mears's remarkable life.

—Marcus Brotherton
Vancouver, Washington
April 2006

Meet Henrietta Mears

She stood about five feet four inches tall, thickset, with hazel eyes dimly visible through the "coke-bottle" lenses of her spectacles. Her daily attire might include a chartreuse dress, a fox fur draped over her shoulders and a hat with a long plume that swept down under her chin. Her gravel voice, considered deep for a woman, resounded when she spoke.[1]

Miss Mears has a deep, expressive voice, full of power. When she speaks and prays, it is truly inspiring. She radiates sunniness both from within and without. This quality even carries over to her dress, which is elegant and attractive. Her enthusiasm and sincerity are abounding. When she speaks, it is from the heart. Her energy seems to be unlimited, and many a college student has grown weary merely trying to keep up with her.[2]

*This woman commanded attention. She was a dynamo, a
seemingly tireless worker with a radiant personality. It was as
if everything she did and everything she said had a purpose.
She spoke with authority in flat, definite declarations bolstered
by facts and her experiences. She had traveled the world several times and seemed to have a tale to tell from every land,
always with a purpose—as an illustration of a Bible truth, a
parallel with the life and teachings of Christ or a manifesta-
tion of what Christian principles could produce. She had a
global view of life and a fully integrated philosophy, mined by
her study, refined by experience and molded and tooled for
her life's purpose: introducing others to Jesus Christ and teaching them to introduce still others to Him, and in the process
influencing the world for Christ.*[3]

CHAPTER 1

Go Big or Go Home

*They're all desperadoes, these kids, all of them
with any life in their veins; the girls as well as the boys;
maybe more than the boys.*

—WARNER FABIAN,
FROM THE ROARING TWENTIES NOVEL *FLAMING YOUTH*

There is always a temptation to think small, to think safe, to do things as they've always been done before.

But not here.

Not in Hollywood.

Not in 1928, the year an unmarried 38-year-old schoolteacher from Minnesota came to town. Henrietta Mears had been hired as the Christian education director of Hollywood First Presbyterian Church. It was an ambitious position for anyone—to reorganize, run and expand a cradle-to-grave Sunday School program for a large-scale church in Southern California. But the time was ripe for casting a huge vision of what could be. This was not a time for thinking small. Hollywood in 1928 was an invitation to magnitude.

Welcome to Opportunity

The climate wasn't always this way. When Hollywood was incorporated as a municipality in 1903, it was a cow town—just a pit stop in the middle of orange groves. The tiny farming town could boast only a post office, a hotel and two markets, along with a population of about 500. Los Angeles, with a population of about 100,000 at the time, seemed far away, separated by trolley lines and slow roads seven miles east through citrus groves. Among the town ordinances in Hollywood was one that outlawed driving cattle through the streets in herds of more than 200. But that was 1903.

Seven years later, in 1910, movie director D. W. Griffith ignited the fuse.

Griffith was sent to Hollywood from the East Coast (where most of the newly formed movie-making companies began) to film a movie. His acting troupe included some of the rising stars of this new industry: Lillian Gish, Mary Pickford and Lionel Barrymore (actress Drew Barrymore's great-uncle). The company couldn't believe Southern California's amazing weather. Where was the snow? The wind? The chilling East Coast rain? They sent letters and telegrams back home raving about their new find.

Several movies were filmed before the troupe returned to New York. By then the secret was out. Word swelled that Hollywood was the thriving climate for this new industry. Directors, production companies, stagehands, agents, actresses and actors descended upon Hollywood. By 1928, Hollywood's population had exploded to more than 36,000. This was the place to go big or go home. Orange groves and agriculture were practically abandoned, replaced by businesses and high-class residences, bungalow courts and apartments.

America greeted this quickly built city with a warm embrace. Almost immediately Hollywood was christened the movie capital of the world. Before television was created, Americans flocked to the theaters. By the early 1920s, 40 million Americans went to the movies each week—and the industry showed no signs of slowing down.

Movies offered Americans a slice of escapism never before seen. Radio had been huge when it first hit—but movies were without comparison. Car chases! Wallops to the head! Fighter pilots dive-bombing the enemy! What an incredible new media! Restrictions were slow to catch up. Movie previews, shown before family-oriented movies, sometimes featured nudity. There were people who fought to restrain the industry, but overall, the movie industry and the city it created could not be daunted. By the end of the decade, about 100 million Americans bought theater tickets every week.

Generation of Fire

This was the city and the social climate in which Henrietta Mears began her new job. If New York was the Big Apple, Hollywood was the Open Mouth. It talked, it sang, it could be kissed or cursed. And oh, how it breathed! Elsewhere in America, movement was still restricted in many ways. But Hollywood was the place to open your lungs, take in a big breath and exhale.

Henrietta knew the incredible challenges and opportunities in front of her: a single woman alone in a new city open to anything. She wrote:

> There is no magic in small plans. When I consider my ministry, I think of the world. Anything less than that would not be worthy of Christ nor of His will for my life.[4]

Several factors were already working in her favor. By 1928, the stage for optimism had been set on a national scale. World War I had been over for 10 years. The war had been about rations, about never having enough, about holding one's self tightly checked. Rationing was now a thing of the past. America wanted to spend, dance, explore—howl. Sales of refrigerators, radios, cookers and telephones boomed. Prices actually fell. Everyone craved a new car. In 1908, the average car cost a staggering $850—out of reach for most Americans. By 1928, the price had plummeted to $290—now everyone could afford one. Cars meant ease of movement and freedom like never before. Nowhere else in America was this more appreciated than Hollywood, whose residents were four times as likely to own a car as the national average, and ten times as likely as Chicago residents.

Henrietta Mears was born into an innovative era, and by the time she came to Hollywood, America had become the wealthiest country in the world, with no obvious rival. Everyone seemed to have money. Just one year later, in 1929, the American stock market would rupture, causing a nationwide depression that had worldwide consequences. But before the crash, optimism seemed endless. In 1928, Republican Herbert Hoover was elected president of the United States, with "a chicken in every pot and a car in every driveway" as his jaunty campaign slogan that promised continued prosperity for the nation.

It was a bright time indeed, when an enterprising young person could really make a mark on the world. America in the 1920s was known as the Jazz Age, the Golden Twenties or the Roaring Twenties. To put this in perspective, if your parents are Baby Boomers, think of Henrietta Mears's generation as the time when your parent's grandparents were young. It was the generation of baseball great Babe Ruth and actor Humphrey Bogart. Laurel and Hardy kept everybody laughing. F. Scott Fitzgerald penned *The Great Gatsby*, a novel about the unrestricted roar of the times.

Freedom for What?

The question could be asked, What was everybody running toward? Passion was high, but passion for what?

With newfound wealth and freedom, young people—especially young women—set themselves free during the Roaring Twenties. They shocked the older generation with their new hairstyle (a short bob). Their clothing often exposed legs and knees. It was not unheard of for the Flappers, as they were called, to wear what was then considered skimpy beachwear and get arrested for indecent exposure. This seldom happened in Hollywood, the place considered the spear point of everything progressive.

Henrietta Mears was not a Flapper, but she always dressed to kill. She especially loved hats. She wore big hats, small hats, a big red cartwheel of a hat, a small red one with a big red rose. There was a hat maker in Buenos Aires who once made 10 different hats for her. One was a fuchsia hat with plumes and another was white with egret feathers. She didn't wear such hats to shock the social norms. It was because she loved pizzazz and sought to honor the Lord with every area of her life—even when wearing a hat.

Practical but progressive, she wrote:

You will attract attention to yourself if you are not abreast of the fashion of the times. If you are properly dressed according to the standard of the group you are in, you can forget yourself. If you are over-dressed, you will feel conspicuous. Be sure every detail is right and then forget your appearance. I think Sunday clothes are a good idea. Why not look your best when you go to church on Sunday? Honoring the Lord should be the greatest occasion of the week.[5]

For a progressive-thinking woman in 1928—spiritually minded or otherwise—there was arguably no better place to be than Hollywood. Elsewhere in America, shocking behavior for a young woman was defined as driving a motorcar, traveling without a male escort, smoking in public, or holding hands with a man without wearing gloves. Mothers formed the Anti-Flirt League to protest these "wild" acts.

But California women were ahead of everything. Already they had fought for and won the right to vote, almost a decade before the nation granted other women the right to do so. Through a variety of organizations—including the Women's Trade Union League of Los Angeles, the Friday Morning Club of Los Angeles, the Women's Socialist League of California and the California Federation of Women's Clubs—women activists played key roles in Progressive Era reforms. They campaigned for the state's pioneering laws: protective labor legislation for women, mothers' pensions, the eight-hour working day and the minimum wage.

By coming to Hollywood when she did, Henrietta Mears had been given a golden key of opportunity. This was a generation open to influence, to change, to progress and to new ideas. The gospel of Christ had always been a radical idea. The challenge now was to know how to engage this culture of passion, to capture its energies for eternal matters, and to set hearts and minds on what was truly most important in life. Could anything good come out of Nazareth? Could Hollywood produce anything spiritual? Henrietta Mears thought so!

The Challenge Before Her

Despite its glitziness and optimism, the Roaring Twenties was an age also known as the Lost Generation, a term first coined by author Gertrude Stein and later made popular by Ernest Hemingway in an epigraph to his novel *The Sun Also Rises*. Henrietta Mears's generation had experienced the horrors of World War I.

It was not uncommon to see veterans in downtown Hollywood with missing arms and legs. Veterans had witnessed horrific new methods of killing, including mustard gas, tanks and trench warfare. Everyone knew someone who hadn't come home alive. The era was characterized by widespread disillusionment. The world had been shaken. What was Truth anymore? The morality and propriety of past Victorian generations didn't seem relevant after the war.

In this environment, it was difficult to find a professor who would admit to the authority of the Scriptures, let alone accept the deity of Christ. One instructor on a state campus began his introductory course in philosophy before some 500 undergraduates by telling them there was no God, and that concept was the very foundation of the course he taught. Now that he had made that clear, they could begin their study of philosophy.

Social dangers and experimentation found fertile soil in this environment. Prohibition had been introduced right after the war ended in 1918. The sale, transportation and making of alcohol became illegal. But America proved to be thirsty, and gangsters provided the sauce. Along with booze came other industries based on deceit, quick money, crime and violence—primarily, illegal taverns (called "speakeasies") and the prostitution they attracted. American cities experienced social climates not unlike the drug wars of today. In 1928, murderous gang bosses achieved stardom. The most famous of all was Al Capone—the gangster boss whose fame rivaled that of Hollywood's superstars. Capone's earnings, primarily through the sale of illegal alcohol, stood at $105 million a year.

Against this Hollywood background, Henrietta's new job as Christian education director at Hollywood First Presbyterian Church was, in a nutshell, to take 450 students and instill something solid, something lasting into their lives. She knew it wouldn't

be an easy job. Though the national climate was primarily opti-
mistic, would a city like Hollywood ever be interested in spiritual
matters? Henrietta wrote of the realities of her new location:

> Hollywood is the most terrible place on the face of the
> earth to organize anything solid, because it is the most
> transient city imaginable. It is a city of make-believe, of
> falsity, of broken homes, of sophistication. Hollywood is
> saturated with insecure people. There is nothing one can
> depend on there.[6]

The job itself was not without hindrances. What validity did
Christian education offer to a church, much less to a nation?
Could she—or anybody, for that matter—ever accomplish any-
thing as a Sunday School teacher? How audacious her dreams!
A doctor perhaps could leave a lasting mark on society; a scien-
tist or a military general or maybe even a movie-maker—but a
Sunday School teacher?!

Sunday School, as an institution, had been around for almost
150 years by 1928; but its vision had blurred from its original
calling of providing biblical schooling for chimney sweeps on
America's East Coast during the Industrial Revolution. Sunday
School was yesterday's vision. Students greeted Henrietta Mears
by telling her, "Sunday School just gets dumber and dumber."
One university student brought up in the church told her that if
he had to pass a test in Bible, he would "absolutely flunk." A few
years later, still in a generation that viewed the institution of
Sunday School as directionless, *Life* magazine described it as "the
most wasted hour in the week."

There was good reason for the concern. As Henrietta glanced
through some of the available curriculum, she saw lessons
geared toward young children with weighty titles such as *Amos*

Denounces Self-Indulgence. (Who wouldn't be spellbound by that?!) Another lesson taught barefaced heresy, suggesting that the apostle Paul survived the shipwreck at Malta (see Acts 27–28) because he had "eaten carrots and was strong." Her research into teaching methodologies and the available curriculum led her to describe the Bible as "the most poorly taught book in the world." Where was the action, the color, the truth, the depth? Where was the passion to know an ever-living, all-powerful, all-amazing Christ?

She saw another problem. Something else was lacking within the Christian community, something that is prone to happen in any organization that predominantly uses volunteers as staff members: Trying to organize a Sunday School to make a lasting difference was like trying to roof a house with cardboard. When rains came, the organization was doomed to leak. Sunday School teachers were untrained and sometimes goaded into service by guilt or necessity. People viewed their service as a duty, not a responsibility. Henrietta wrote:

> How seldom the Sunday School teacher is asked for his credentials! A public school teacher is not questioned as to whether he will teach but rather, can he teach. Our request in securing Sunday School teachers is invariably, "Will you take a class?" And good-natured men and women, much against their wills, answer, "I will keep the class going until you can find someone else." If a math teacher is absent, can you imagine the principal going out in the neighborhood, ringing doorbells and asking a housewife, "Will you come over and take a class in mathematics because the regular teacher is sick?" Absurd! He notifies the superintendent's office of his need, and a trained person comes.[7]

Oh, and by the way, when she first arrived at the church, there was no Christian education building.

Her career stretched out before her like a broad, unmarked highway. Where could Henrietta Mears possibly begin?

What You Are Called to Do, You Become

How tempting it was to lick a stamp.

"Don't do that," said Ethel May Baldwin, Henrietta Mears's personal secretary and assistant in the Christian education office at Hollywood First Presbyterian Church. Ethel May's job was to be responsible for most of the administrative work in the department—the scheduling for counseling appointments, speaking, meetings and committees, and keeping the concentric circles in motion. She could run interference as capably as a UCLA fullback.

"Please put down the stamp," Ethel May repeated to Henrietta, shortly after Henrietta arrived on the job. "We can do that for you. Hundreds of others can do that for you. You do what the rest of us can't do."

Henrietta set down the stamp, rolled up her sleeves, and began to tackle the complexity of her new job.

She wrote:

> The first thing I did in Hollywood was to write out what I wanted for my Sunday School. I set down my objectives for the first five years. They included improvements in organization, teaching staff, curriculums, and spirit. I wanted a closely graded program, a teaching material that would present Christ and his claims in every lesson, a trained teaching staff, a new education building, choirs, clubs, a camp program, a missionary vision, youth trained for the hour.[8]

Something in that commonsense formula took hold. Within a few years, her Sunday School grew from 450 students to more than 6,000. An editorial in the *Sunday School Times* encouraged pastors and leaders who were concerned about their own dwindling congregations to go to Hollywood First Presbyterian Church and see what was happening.

So something worked.

Henrietta remained in her role of Christian education director at the church for 35 years, during which time her job description expanded into the following list of responsibilities and achievements:

- Teach the college-age Sunday School class with eventually more than 500 on the active roll. The group would constantly change, so her audience was continually new. This group met Sunday mornings for class, Sunday evenings for college hour, and Wednesday nights for prayer meetings, with parties, deputation (ministry) groups, conferences and retreats in between. Henrietta needed to counsel, supervise, train her leaders and present a continuing challenge in her teaching.

- Organize and recruit leaders to oversee the high school and junior high as well as the Ambassador group—the business and professional young people just above college age. Oversee superintendents and directors for Sunday School departments for all other ages in the church. This included nursery, children, young married groups, Homebuilders, Mariners, Voyagers and Harvesters. For all of these groups, the leadership had to be trained, the teaching materials coordinated and all personnel supervised in a Sunday School that eventually consisted of 18 departments.

- Continual planning for summer conferences, Sunday School calling days (contacting people), camps, vacation Bible schools, the summer program and the "Sings" (corporate times of singing hymns and choruses) that took place after the Sunday evening church service.
- Oversee the administration and overall direction for the foreign and home deputation (ministry) teams. Every summer teams would go to Europe, the Orient, Alaska and to the migrant camps of the United States. Henrietta would also be a member of the candidate committee to interview young people going into vocational Christian work, including candidates for the ministry. More than 400 young people from the college department would eventually go into vocational Christian work. Ministers and missionaries who had responded to Henrietta's influence would be scattered over the face of the map: in the United States cities of Seattle, Sacramento, San Diego, Los Angeles, New Jersey, Colorado, Montana; throughout the world—the Belgian Congo, Tokyo, Thailand, India, Ethiopia, French Cameroon, Philippines, Formosa, Australia, France, Denmark, China, Germany, and countless other places.
- Develop summer internship programs for seminary students.
- Oversee the building of three large Christian education buildings at the church, all the while continuing classes and finding places for the growing number of students to meet.
- Speak at conferences all over the world.
- Write curriculum.
- Write books.

- Start a publishing company.
- Start a conference center.
- Start an international curriculum company.

Historians credit Henrietta Mears with changing the face of a generation. Wherever she labored—before audiences of thousands throughout the English-speaking world; within the Sunday School she built to be one of the largest in the world; at Forest Home Christian Conference Center, which she founded; among the stars of Hollywood, whom she befriended; or through her numerous writings, which are still in print to this day—she was an open lifeline of power. Her contribution to the international cause of the gospel ranks as one of the most important and influential in the twentieth century.

"Teach the Word clearly and correctly," Henrietta Mears always said, "to the end that people may come to know Christ as Savior and Lord and to grow spiritually, faithful in every good work."

There's always a temptation to think small, to think safe, to do things as they've always been done before.

How necessary it was to dream big from the start.

CHAPTER 2

But She Went On

*Will you stop looking at your problems and
wringing your hands in despair?
Faith and despair cannot remain in the same heart.*[1]
*Take your choice; trust God or worry.
You cannot really do both.*[2]

—HENRIETTA MEARS

The twenty-first century is an age of recovery. We've all been hurt at some time: maybe our parents divorced, or perhaps we struggle with an addiction. It's easy to weigh a life by its painful circumstances. We can give in to the temptation to think that overcoming the difficult things of life—experiencing victory—is not possible. Yes, Christ offers us eternal salvation, but life in the meantime, plagued by burdens or our troubled upbringing, seems to be one of survival only.

Henrietta Mears would consider that line of thinking garbage.

It's not that she didn't have compassion for hurting people. It's that her belief system pushed far beyond despair and contained something much more powerful than optimism. She had a huge faith. She believed that God is a God of action, of strength, of results, of change. Victory for her meant completely trusting God at His word and then rolling up her sleeves and working hard—no matter what happened in life. "Nothing less than our best for Christ," she wrote, "and nothing more than God's complete adequacy for our inadequacy."

Henrietta had her share of painful circumstances as a child and young adult, yet she was single-minded in her quest to live an amazing life for Jesus Christ. About her aims to develop character and personality, she wrote:

> When I was a teenager, I heard my mother say of a rather nondescript fellow, "When he walks into the room, you are not aware that anyone has come in. You think, rather, that the wind has blown the door open." That trenchant criticism cut into my mind and made me think of the type of person I was, and I resolved that I was going to be different, that people would not think that just the wind blew the door open when I walked into the room. And so I began to ask myself, "What makes an interesting personality? How can I develop my personality so I will be able to attract men and women to Christ?" The Lord's promise seemed to summarize everything that I was thinking: "I have come, that they might have life, and that they might have it more abundantly" (John 10:10).
>
> I think of Jesus as vital, alert, enthusiastic—full of zest and zeal. So much emphasis is placed on the suffering and dying Christ—and certainly that is essential—but rarely do we see paintings or hear sermons that reflect the vitality of Christ's personality and the life He wants us to have. Christ is the ideal leader—men leave their professions, their homes, their companions to follow Him. He inspired them to do their best, to be their highest self. Jesus must have been a physically vibrant person, radiating energy and confidence,

mental alertness and interest in everything about Him. Think of Him being able to speak to a crowd of many thousands of people—without a microphone! See Him walking through cities, His head high, His shoulders thrown back, bursting with good will, kindness, courage and faith! No wonder the multitudes followed Him![3]

Joy and Sorrow, Abundance and Pain

Opportunities and obstacles—Henrietta experienced both while growing up. Her parents, Ashley and Margaret Mears, knew both luxury and sorrow and didn't hide the family from either. They moved their family from Chicago and settled in Fargo, North Dakota, shortly before Henrietta Cornelia Mears was born October 23, 1890. Ashley owned a chain of 20 banks across the Dakotas, and the move west helped him to be closer to his business. Henrietta's parents were financially able to indulge her every need for the first three years of her life. She even had her own nurse, Tillie, as a constant companion.

Then the Great Panic of 1893 hit. Four years of disastrous depression followed. Railways collapsed; silver-mining and agriculture states, particularly in the West, encountered economic ruin; businesses failed; construction all but stopped; and banks across the country closed, including many owned by Henrietta's father. This setback in the family's financial stability caused Henrietta later in life to joke, "I was born with a silver spoon in my mouth, but it was yanked out before I got the taste of it."

Henrietta was too young to know all that was happening. The youngest of the family, she was tiny and energetic, the delight of her parents and adored by her older brothers and her sister, Margaret. Henrietta managed to keep the entire household on its toes. She was a welcomed child, celebrated in many ways and loved unconditionally by her family. That would be important to her future, because in addition to economic setbacks, the family experienced its share of personal tragedy.

Ashley and Margaret's first son, Ashley Jr., died suddenly on his twentieth birthday. Will, their second son, came down with spinal meningitis at 14 and was deaf for the rest of his life. The birth of Clarence, their third son, was followed by the birth of a daughter, Florence, who died at age 7 from typhoid. Fifth in the family line was son Norman; then came Margaret. Margaret was 11 years old, and her mother 42, when Henrietta, the family's seventh and last child was born.

Hardships can leave their mark on a family. When Florence died, Henrietta's mother described the experience as feeling like "the whole world drained out through a small hole and left nothing." It was then that Christ became her all. From that time on, Henrietta's mother's life was completely devoted to God's work. This spiritual legacy would not go unnoticed. One day, young Henrietta saw her mother go to her room, and she followed. Henrietta found her mother on her knees, hands folded and lips moving in prayer. The praying lasted for an hour.

Henrietta noticed that her mother did this every day. So one morning, Henrietta got the family's large alarm clock, placed it on the bedspread in front of her and closed her eyes, determined to follow her mother's example. She prayed and prayed and prayed. She prayed for everything she could think of. She would pause and think and pray some more. When she peeked at the clock to see how she was doing, only one minute had elapsed. What did her mother think of to pray for a whole hour?

Sometime during Henrietta's first few years of life, the Mears family moved from North Dakota to Duluth, Minnesota, for a brief time before settling in Minneapolis. The family regularly attended the First Baptist Church of Minneapolis, which was pastored by Dr. W. B. Riley, a Bible scholar who became nationally known through his powerful preaching, evangelism and eventual writing of several books.

A Child's Serious Belief

Like many young children who have yet to begin school, Henrietta longed to go to kindergarten, and counted off the days until she was old enough to go. But on the first day, she returned home with a disgusted look on her face. "Kindergarten is to amuse little children," she told her mother. "I'm amused enough. I want to be educated."

She had a keen mind and a natural instinct for wanting to see things accomplished at once. Church fascinated her. She used to rush home from school and take a nap—that was the only way her mother would allow her to attend evening services at church. She became a Christian at age 7, a decision she made on her own, and she sought baptism and church membership as a reflection of her commitment. A cousin of about the same age, Margaret Buckbee Greig, was baptized along with her. As was common in their church, before their baptism the girls stood before the congregation and responded to questions about faith and doctrine. The girls answered with such clarity and frankness that the congregation broke out in laughter. Henrietta, thinking that she was saying something wrong, turned in dismay to her mother, who encouraged the girls to keep going.

Henrietta knew firsthand that children are capable of understanding deep issues of the faith, so why would people think it funny? As an adult, she wrote of the importance of seriously targeting every age in the church, even infants:

Do you have a place for every age in your Sunday School?
And do you have a program for every age? And is your program as good as it could be? I detest paper cradle rolls!
Little booties hung up on the wall with little pink ribbons—
I despise the horrible things! We have just finished an educational building for our babies including children up
through the primary department. We spent half a million
dollars on babies! One of the elders raised his eyebrows and
asked if such a building was necessary for "just the babies."
I told him that such a building was the most necessary
structure in the world; for if the parents have a place to put
the babies, they will come with their children and in turn
go to the young marrieds' class. Thus we have a Sunday
School atmosphere from the very beginning. Besides that,
our psychologists and educators tell us that we have no
idea what impressions are made on little children: beautiful
music, lovely colors, stories. We have learned to condition
them to love the house of the Lord.[4]

Henrietta's mother was interested in social justice and frequently visited homes of the poor and invalid. When she felt that
Henrietta was old enough to understand the importance of compassion toward others, she took her daughter with her on these visits.
Henrietta met with the sick and the hurting, giving them little gifts,
or praying with them. When Henrietta was 10, she and her cousin
Margaret formed a service club called "The Willing Workers," whose
mission statement was "To do good for unfortunates."

Time was always a premium value in the Mears's household.
Henrietta's mother would not allow her children to sleep late,
even on holidays. Summer vacation was not for "running wild all
day"—mornings were spent in reading, memorizing great literature or practicing music. During school months, any homework

needed to be finished by Friday evening so that weekends would not be haunted by the anxiety of having procrastinated Monday morning's homework assignments.

Henrietta's mother would sometimes come up to one of her children who was reading, close the book and ask, "What are you learning?"

Once Henrietta said, "But Mother, I've only been reading for 10 minutes."

"My dear," said Henrietta's mother, "if you've been reading that long, you certainly should have learned something by now. Now tell me what you have read."

Another time, Henrietta returned home from a party, complaining that it was boring.

"Well, what did *you* do to make it interesting?" her mother asked. "Wasn't there some game you could have suggested? Even though it wasn't your party, you should have felt an obligation to help the others have a good time."

Perhaps she didn't learn the lesson on social responsibility soon enough. When Henrietta returned from a church youth meeting with the same complaint, her mother said, "But did *you* give a testimony, Henrietta? Did you offer to help plan the meeting?"

This training developed in Henrietta a sense of responsibility, initiative and purpose that would serve her well throughout her life.

At age 11, she taught her first Sunday School class. From that moment on, she knew that her God-given abilities and ambitions would find their greatest fulfillment in drawing others toward a life-changing relationship with Christ.

The Blows Rain Down

When Henrietta was 12, she began to notice a strange pain in her joints. Soon the pain was constant and she was unable to walk.

She became almost completely immobile and had to be carried from place to place. She also began having heavy nosebleeds. When doctors were called, Henrietta was diagnosed with muscular rheumatism, a potentially crippling and life-threatening disease. Other cases were reported in the region that year, and one of her friends also contracted the disease and died from it.

For two years Henrietta lay sick. Various treatments were pursued, but nothing seemed to work. One day, when Henrietta's mother was reading Philippians 4:19—"But my God shall supply all your needs according to his riches in glory by Christ Jesus"— she claimed that promise for her daughter and asked a family friend and devout believer, Mr. Ingersoll, to come and pray for Henrietta's healing.

"Henrietta, do you believe the Lord can heal you?" Mr. Ingersoll asked.

Henrietta's direct response was, "He created us. I see no reason why He cannot heal us."

Mr. Ingersoll prayed; the nosebleeds stopped immediately. But the rheumatism continued, even becoming more painful.

Mr. Ingersoll was called to the Mears home again. This time as he prayed, Henrietta was filled with a sudden and unmistakable confidence. She began to cry when she knew she was completely healed. The pain was gone—abruptly and miraculously gone! Out loud, while surrounding the bed where she lay, her family praised God and thanked Him for healing Henrietta. Her road to full recovery was swift and complete. She became more active, building up her muscles by working in the garden, swimming and horseback riding. Within three months, her body was free of any trace of the illness, and she never had a recurrence of rheumatism.

Her eyesight, however, was another matter. Henrietta's eyes had never been strong. She was so nearsighted that she wore glasses from age 6. When she was 16, she accidentally jabbed a hat pin into the pupil of one eye. Her doctors could do nothing to heal it and predicted that she would be blind in that eye by age 30. Mr. Ingersoll came once more to pray for Henrietta's eye. She had no doubt that the God who had made her could also heal her. When specialists later examined her eye, they agreed there was indeed a hole in the pupil but shook their heads in amazement that Henrietta could still see. For more than two years they periodically examined her to see if her sight was declining; but even though they could find no change, they remained unconvinced that a miracle had taken place.

"You need to stop reading and studying," doctors warned her as high school graduation approached. "You will completely lose your sight even sooner."

Henrietta planned to attend university. With this grim prediction from her doctors, would she still be able to go? The decision was hers, her parents told her.

Her decision came without hesitation. "If I'm going to go blind by 30, then blind I shall be. But I want something in my head to think about. I'm going to study as hard as I can for as long as I can."

As a freshman at the University of Minnesota, Henrietta plunged into her studies and into Christian service, becoming Sunday School superintendent of the junior department at church. Always aware of her fragile eye condition, but desiring to continue in school and in her church ministry, she practiced her powers of concentration during lectures and made the most of her study times, resolving to study only during daylight hours. Immediately after every class she would prepare for the next day's lessons. She always finished each assignment while the subject was fresh in her mind. Her powers of concentration and her memory developed so strongly that she could fully grasp the content of a textbook in a single reading. She could remember and repeat almost verbatim nearly all that she heard in each lecture. Later, when asked about her lifelong struggle with her eyes, Henrietta said:

> I believe my greatest spiritual asset throughout my entire life has been my failing sight, for it has kept me absolutely dependent upon God.[5]

A Final Blow

On a winter's night, in the cold stillness of her college dorm room, Henrietta, age 20, had never felt such loneliness in her life. Her studies were the furthest thing from her mind right then. She didn't want to go out with friends or talk to anyone; she just wanted to be alone.

Just a week before, on December 29, 1910, Henrietta's world had changed irrevocably when her mother—her mentor, teacher, strength and friend—died. The funeral was held December 31. The chapel had been packed with mourners; many of them had spoken of her service and influence. Henrietta's mother was buried in Chicago the next day. A newspaper obituary, written by the family's pastor, Dr. Riley, read:

> Mrs. Mears left her husband, C. Ashley Mears, three sons and two daughters, Margaret and Henrietta. As a Bible teacher she had few equals in the city of Minneapolis, and in the practice of the presence of God she had no superior. The church is poorer for her going but rich in her ministry and in the influence certain to abide forever.[6]

Henrietta's grief filled her tiny dorm room as snow swirled in the darkness outside. When she thought of what Dr. Riley had said to her at the funeral, "Henrietta, I am praying that your mother's spiritual mantle will fall upon you," she wondered how she would go on, much less continue her mother's ministries. An open Bible lay before her. In the stillness, it seemed as if a Voice spoke. Henrietta wrote of the experience:

> I felt absolutely powerless from the thought that I could possibly live up to what my mother had been and had done, and I prayed that if God had anything for me to do that He would supply the power. I read my Bible for every reference to the Holy Spirit and His power. The greatest realization came to me when I saw that there was nothing I had to do to receive His power, but to submit to Christ, to allow him to control me.
>
> I had been trying to do everything myself; now I let Christ take me completely. I said to Christ that if He wanted anything from me that He would have to do it Himself. My life was changed from that moment on.[7]

That was it. In that moment in her dorm room, it seemed as if Henrietta's entire life narrowed down to her relationship with the Lord, as though the doorway was so small that only she and the Lord could go through it—a "needle's eye" experience in faith.

Her mother had always fixed baskets for the poor at Christmastime, and Henrietta had gone with her to do the shopping. They always bought butter and jelly as well as food staples. "The Lord doesn't just give dry bread, you know," her mother would say. "And we will put in milk and cream, too, for the Lord gives extra things."

One year later, the first Christmas after her mother's death, Henrietta and Margaret went shopping for the baskets and invited poor and hurting guests to their home for Christmas.

On their search to find guests, they found a family of children whose mother was away from home working as a laundress to make a living. An eight-year-old child had been left in charge, caring for a three-year-old boy and a baby, who was tethered to the clothesline for safekeeping. Henrietta and Margaret took the children shopping and invited them to their home for Christmas dinner.

"Please fix the table with the finest silver and linen," Henrietta told the maid. "We're entertaining the Lord, you know."

For this small family of children, the finest foods were prepared that Christmas. Dessert was pudding piled high with whipped cream. When it was served, the children looked at it with big serious eyes. The three-year-old burst into tears, his grief inconsolable.

"My pudding's ruined," he wailed. "It's got soapsuds all over it!"

Henrietta encouraged him to taste it. When he cautiously spooned up a bite, his eyes became huge.

"These are the best-tasting soapsuds I ever had," he said.[8]

But She Went On

Sometimes deep spiritual comprehension comes through times of loss or the death of a loved one. That dark night in her dorm room seemed to conclude Henrietta's childhood and launch her into adult life and ministry with newfound strength and vitality. Already her life had been marked by joy and sorrow, luxury and pain. By the time she was 20, she had lost two siblings and her mother—her father would soon follow. One of her brothers was deaf. She had been sick for two years, and then healed. Her eyesight was a constant liability.

But still she went on with strength and purpose.

Early evidence of what the Holy Spirit would do in and through Henrietta's life came the year following her mother's death. She started a Bible study for women in the university's

Shevlin Hall. The class met each Thursday; she was the sole teacher. Only a few young women attended at first, but those few began bringing their friends. Soon, 60 young women studied and prayed together. Henrietta continued the class through the end of her senior year. Several women from that class later went into missionary service.

When Henrietta graduated from university in 1913, her amazing adult life had begun its unstoppable, determined course.

CHAPTER 3

Becoming

*And Jesus grew in wisdom and stature, and in
favor with God and men.*

LUKE 2:52

I f you examine the résumé of any great person, you will usu-
ally find that he or she filled several positions that were less
than great. For example, King David began as a shepherd.
Joseph was a slave before he rose to second-in-command over
all of Egypt. The early, less-than-great times in our lives are the
training ground for developing character, strength and perseverance—for developing resilience and good decision-making
ability.

It can be easy to forget the end goal when you're on the less-
than-great side of a calling. You may have a college degree but
are waiting tables in a restaurant. Or perhaps you've just begun
on the bottom rung of a company and can't see a time when
you'll be able to step up the ladder. Maybe you're a new mother,
knee-deep in diapers. Or you're just beginning a work that
requires a long season of paying dues. Where's the glory in this?
Where's the significance, the sense of calling?

In many ways, Henrietta Mears began her life's calling in
1928, at age 38, when she took the job as director of Christian
education for the Hollywood First Presbyterian Church. What

had she done before then? What were the positions along the way that helped shape and mold the skills and abilities she would use in her ultimate calling? How did she, like Jesus, grow in wisdom and stature and favor with God and men? Like David, Joseph, Moses, and a host of others, Henrietta paid her dues in several early roles in which she learned lessons that formed the foundation of what was to come. She committed herself to God's plan, no matter what.

Henrietta recognized the benefit of starting small, of humbling herself before the Lord so that He could lift her up in His timing (see Jas. 4:10). She also recognized the value of pursuing huge dreams. There was a season of preparation, but there was always a goal to influence others for Christ. For her, only an amazing life for Christ would do. She wrote:

> So many people are willing to be bellhops for the Lord, standing around waiting for someone to give them some little errand to do for Him, instead of asking the Lord to give them His greatest will for their lives. There are so few who want to do the big things for God. You should not be content to pump the organ if God wants you to play on it.[1]

A Schoolteacher's Influence

After Henrietta graduated college in 1913, she moved to Beardsley, Minnesota, to teach school. Beardsley wasn't even remotely like Hollywood. Located about 90 miles from Fargo, and 240 miles from Minneapolis, Beardsley had a population of about 850 (since then the population has shrunk to about 250). Most of the town's men spent their time loafing at the pool hall. Henrietta found the morals of the area so appalling that she commented, "God made the country, man the city, and the devil the small town." Henrietta served the high school as both chemistry teacher and principal, and taught speech and dramatics as sideline responsibilities.

Whatever her role, she determined to be a positive influence on her students. She coached plays, organized choirs and raised money for a new piano. When she discovered that the school had no football team, she organized one and recruited a coach. The team played during the off-seasons in the farming community, which often meant playing in sleet or mud. Henrietta never missed a game, cheering on her school's team from the bench.

Henrietta volunteered to teach a young people's Bible class in the town's Methodist church. She invited her football team to attend, and they often filled the first rows. Few members of the Beardsley church had much to give that year when the annual missions campaign to raise money for missionaries was announced. But Henrietta challenged her class to bring in as much money as they could. Somehow she created a matching plan that further inspired the students. Townspeople were shocked to see her class running errands, doing extra chores and tackling odd jobs for cash. When missionary Sunday arrived, the Sunday School classes reported their collections: $1.25, $3.00, $15.50. Then the minister called out, "Miss Mears's Young People's Class."

Charlie—one of the hardest working members of Henrietta's class—leaped to his feet and shouted, "One hundred twenty dollars!"

Soon after, two football players approached Henrietta, asking her to start an additional Bible class for the team. She agreed that on the condition they would invite the rest of their friends. The class was held in the living room of the home where she lived. As the weeks passed, attendance grew and the living room was filled to capacity. The students overflowed to the hallway and up the stairs. Finally, they opened the windows of the living room so the kids who couldn't get in could stand outside and listen.

Before Henrietta's year in Beardsley ended, a Catholic priest called on her to thank her for the amazing changes he was seeing through her efforts in the lives of the town's young people and the whole community.

But there was more that happened that year—there came an opportunity to meet someone.

One night, a group of Beardsley's teachers attended a corn-husking party at a large farm. Henrietta was introduced to a young man whose parents owned the town's hotel. He was a Harvard graduate, good looking and a good conversationalist. Henrietta found herself drawn to him. He asked if he could take her home after the party. She said yes. For two furious weeks their friendship grew. They went for long drives in the countryside and dined out together. One day the president of the school board called on Henrietta. His brow was furrowed as he spoke to her directly in a low voice, saying,

"What kind of young man is he, Miss Mears?"

"Why, just wonderful," Henrietta answered. "He is very intelligent, gracious, polite—very charming in every way."

"Well, I always knew that someone, some day would find a good side to him," said the school board president. "The trouble is that he has such a bad reputation that if you continue going with him the town simply will not believe that you are reforming him. You see, he has the worst reputation in town. I always felt he had possibilities, but it seemed there was never anyone to challenge him. But you will ruin your reputation instead of improving his."[2]

Henrietta was stunned, dismayed, almost in disbelief of what she heard. Here was a young man who seemed to be everything she was looking for. Eligible men were few and far between in Beardsley. These were the days before convenient long-distance travel and communication. If she said no to the young man's pursuit, what would it mean for her future? Yet, unable to doubt the school board president's counsel, she knew she needed to act on what he had told her. Marrying the wrong person because you don't want to be single only creates more problems.

That night, when the young man called on her, she told him they could not continue to see each other.

"I know what you've heard," he said. "The trouble is, it's true. I know it would be too much to try to live down, so I'm going to leave town. I didn't care until I met you. Now I'm sorry."

"It's too bad that you didn't have enough courage to be true to yourself," Henrietta said gently.

"I know," he said. "I want to make a fresh start. At least I want to thank you for making me want to start over again somewhere else."[3]

And then he was gone, leaving town abruptly. Some days later, the young man's mother visited Henrietta and thanked her for giving her son a reason to change and for inspiring him to become something better.

Correct as the decision was, Henrietta was still alone.

Another Choice

The Beardsley school year ended, and another teaching position opened, this time in North Branch, a slightly larger small town about 230 miles from Beardsley. Again, Henrietta worked as the chemistry teacher and principal at the high school. Again she volunteered at the Methodist church with Sunday School and youth groups. She poured her energy into work and church.

While in North Branch, Henrietta was again tested in the matter of a romantic relationship. The attraction proved more difficult this time, but ultimately drew her to a place where she knew what the Lord really wanted her to do. She would say later that this was the only young man she had ever loved and fully considered marrying.

He was a young banker—tall, handsome, black-haired, intellectually challenging and socially proficient. He was unlike most anyone else in the small town. He was a graduate of Dartmouth and had traveled extensively. Since North Branch was a small town, she couldn't walk down the street without running into him. If she went into the post office, there he was. A trip to the drugstore would bring an unexpected meeting—and so the friendship developed rapidly.

Yet as they grew closer, Henrietta sensed that something was wrong in their friendship. Maybe she could handle it in such a way that the issue need never be faced. Once, when he was out of town on a business trip, a young dentist asked Henrietta to go out with him. She had several dates with the dentist and was sure this would discourage the banker's enthusiasm. But her seeing the dentist only brought matters to a head more quickly. When the banker returned, he asked Henrietta to marry him.

There was something in their relationship, however, that made Henrietta question her faith. Exactly what the problem was is not recorded, but somehow they were not on the same page spiritually. He tried to make her see that he admired her religious convictions. He tried to persuade her that they could establish their home and that she could go on and believe and do just as she wanted and not change in any way. A home was very important to Henrietta. She loved children and companionship; she loved entertaining and social life; and she loved the young man doing the persuading. Yet she knew that a serious relationship with him would ultimately compromise her faith and beliefs.

As the months slipped by, Henrietta could not escape the thought that marrying this man, as fine as he was, would be like establishing a home and deciding that each night the husband would dine in one room and the wife in another. They would both have an excellent meal, but they would have no fellowship together. If in matters of faith they could not sit at the same table and agree, their relationship would be impossible. It was the time of her greatest decision. Again she knelt in prayer, this time on a Minnesota spring night, and prayed in solitude:

> Lord, you have made me the way I am. I love a home, I love security, I love children, and I love him. Yet I feel that marriage under these conditions would draw me away from You. I surrender, Lord, even this, and I leave it in Your hands. Lead me, Lord, and strengthen me. You have promised to fulfill all my needs. I trust in You.[4]

For Henrietta, the matter was now settled. She knew what she had to do, and she did it. She ended the relationship.

Again, correct as the decision was, she was still alone.

No other mention of dating is ever found in Henrietta's life story. Later in life she joked that the apostle Paul was the only man she could have married, but he didn't wait for her. When she taught about the woman at the well who had five husbands, Henrietta would laugh wryly and say: "Now, she must have been a real glamour girl. She could get five husbands, and I couldn't get one."

Single though she remained, the matter must have been settled in her mind. Much later she wrote:

> The marvelous thing has been that the Lord has always given me a beautiful home; He has given me thousands of children; He has supplied every need in my life, and I've never felt lonely. Since I am a very gregarious person, I thought I would have a feeling that I didn't belong. But I've never had it, never! I've never missed companionship.
>
> Through one experience after another the Lord has shown me that He had something special for me to do. After I went through that final door, where it was just the Lord and me, into wide open spaces of people and things and excitement, life has been one great adventure. It has been a tremendous thing to see how the Lord has filled my life so abundantly with lovely things, and I want to tell everyone that where the Lord puts you—even alone on an island—He absolutely satisfies you.
>
> So often young people will say to me, "Oh, Miss Mears, I want to be just like you! You are so happy! I, too, never want to get married."
>
> And I say to them, "Nonsense! The Lord intends for you to marry; that is the way He has made us. It just so happens that in my case that wasn't His will."
>
> But it has pleased me to know that young people have been able to see my happiness and my complete satisfaction in the life that God has given me.[5]

An Unexpected Home

Henrietta's teaching contract in North Branch ended after one year and she made plans to return to Minneapolis. But North Branch was not prepared to let her go so easily. When she arrived at the railway station for her train to the city, a delegation from the school board intercepted her and made a final effort with a tempting offer to keep her in town. They offered her a new contract and bonus to remain. But she was certain the Lord was leading her elsewhere, and she returned to Minneapolis.

That fall she taught chemistry at a junior high school in Minneapolis. She wanted to teach at a high school level, but the Minneapolis school board declined her application, believing that she was too young to teach high school in a large city (even though she had already taught high school for two years—as well as been a school principal—in two small towns). She accepted the junior high post on a substitute basis only; she had trained to teach high school students and that was what she wanted to do. She would not accept a permanent position on any other level.

A year later, she was offered a position to teach mathematics at Central High School in Minneapolis. She wanted to teach chemistry, but because she was being offered a high school teaching position, she accepted. On the first day of school, the principal announced that the regular chemistry teacher had been drafted into the military. Henrietta was put on the regular staff of the high school as chemistry teacher and held that position for the next 10 years. Eventually she became head of the chemistry department and was appointed senior class advisor.

Henrietta soon became involved in teaching Sunday School again. At the First Baptist Church, her sister, Margaret, had been teaching a class of 18-year-old girls who called themselves (much to Margaret's horror) The Snobs. True to their name, The Snobs didn't permit outsiders to join their class. Margaret asked Henrietta to take over the class. Henrietta rolled up her sleeves and went to work. Within a few months, the group stopped calling themselves The Snobs. The girls caught the vision that church is not a club for exclusivity; it is a place of community and service. When the Sunday School was reorganized, all the former Snobs except one took teaching and service positions in the church!

Henrietta was left with only one student, a girl who had been to the Sunday School class only once before. The two of them set out to canvass the neighborhood. They called on every home within a mile of the church. The following Sunday, 55 girls showed up.

The class met in the same small room The Snobs had once occupied, but attendance soon doubled. Over the years they pushed out the walls of every room they occupied. Within a decade, the class had more than 500 members. An additional hall was built to house them. As an outgrowth of this class, Henrietta organized a service group of young women to work on projects for missionaries. Of the class, Henrietta wrote, "If a project has a purpose, and that purpose is never forgotten but continually fulfilled, then 'the light shines in the darkness and nothing shall put it out.'"

In Minneapolis, sisters Henrietta and Margaret bought a house together. Margaret, who was 11 years older than Henrietta, had been a successful businesswoman in their brother's firm for over 20 years. She sensed God's hand on Henrietta's life and realized that her younger sister was marked for great ministry. She devoted the rest of her life to her sister's care by encouraging her and running the household. She paid the bills and did the shopping—even picking out and purchasing all of Henrietta's clothes.

Margaret had a keen, practical approach to life and a sharp, dry wit. A marvelous hostess and the frequent preparer of large meals, she playfully referred to the church dining hall as "The Royal

Gorge." She frequently invited people into their home for a meal or to stay for a few days. The sisters' home was a center for the humble and distinguished alike. The home was beautifully ordered and was ready for a visitor at any time, and everyone felt at home. It was a good physical background for Henrietta's spiritual career: The atmosphere was always uplifting, peaceful, and a contrast to all the serious issues that Henrietta constantly had to face.

The Call Is Set

Toward the end of Henrietta's high school teaching career, a childhood friend and missionary, Evelyn Camp, came home on her first furlough from Japan. She described her experiences in Japan to Henrietta's large Sunday School class. Henrietta had once seriously considered going to Japan as a missionary herself, but now she knew why the Lord had called her elsewhere. Her calling was to train leaders and to nurture the spiritual growth of people who could go in her place to penetrate the world with the gospel of Christ. Henrietta would be only one person going to Japan, but God had called her to multiply herself in the lives of others He would send out in her place.

Henrietta believed that God calls individuals to specific places and to a specific work. Too many people look at a need first instead of looking at the Lord. A need speaks, but there are thousands of needs and thousands of places, so God must call you to the one place, to the one work He wants you to do. She also believed that God does not call you to do something you don't want to do: First He renews your mind and gives you the desire to do that work; then He helps you do it. She wrote:

/

> If you're afraid God is going to call you to China, forget
> all about that. There are so many people in China now

they probably don't want one more. I thought China was the only place God would call me; and when He didn't, I wondered what was wrong! God will lead you and give you the desire in your heart for the one place He wants you to fill.[6]

In 1927, after several years of teaching at Central High, Henrietta took a sabbatical leave. She was at a critical juncture in her life. She had to decide whether she was to continue teaching in the high school or choose another field. If she remained in teaching, it was time for her to go to Columbia University to prepare for administration work. She remembered so vividly the night she had given her life to Christ for vocational Christian work, when she was 17; but God had not called her to the mission field. Now the one thought uppermost in her mind and heart was to find the definite place and work where God wanted her to serve.

The need to decide had been precipitated by a visitor from California. This one visitor would change Henrietta's life—and the lives of literally millions of others—forever.

CHAPTER 4

It Begins

*Many are the plans in a man's heart, but it is
the Lord's purpose that prevails.*

PROVERBS 19:22

It started out as just another average Sunday. Henrietta and
Margaret went to their church in Minneapolis, expecting to
see their pastor, Dr. Riley, in the pulpit. But he was out of town.
In his place was Dr. Stewart MacLennan, a guest speaker from
the Hollywood First Presbyterian Church. He had a tall, brilliant presence in the pulpit. He preached eloquently, fearlessly
and movingly. That morning he preached on the love of Christ,
and his sermon made a profound impact on the two sisters.

Margaret and Henrietta often invited visiting ministers to
Sunday lunch, but this time Henrietta said to one of the deacons, "I don't think it's fair for us always to have the privilege of fellowshipping with these guests. Why don't you take
Dr. MacLennan to your home today?"

The deacon refused. "Now, Henrietta," he said, "you know
they always have a better time with you and Margaret."

So Dr. MacLennan went to Sunday lunch with the Mears sisters. After about two hours of food and conversation, Henrietta
suggested they should drive him back to his hotel so that he
could rest and prepare for the evening's service.

"Actually, I'd rather stay," said the pastor. "You see, I'm writing a new series of sermons on the person of Christ, and I would like very much to go over them with you."

Henrietta and Dr. MacLennan discussed the sermons throughout the afternoon. When it was time to leave, he invited the sisters to come and visit Hollywood if they were ever in California. The sisters just laughed. The idea was so unexpected. (These were the days before widespread air travel.) Besides, they were settled in Minnesota, with good jobs and a house. California seemed like the end of the earth.

On that Sunday, Henrietta Mears and Dr. MacLennan from the Hollywood First Presbyterian Church met and parted. Though they would not realize it, their meeting was a pivotal point for the twentieth-century evangelical church. History was being made.

Just another average Sunday.

Finding God's Will

Henrietta arranged to take a year's sabbatical from teaching at Central High, and she and her sister left for Europe. As they traveled and saw the sights, they sought the Lord's will in what was to come next: continued work in public schools for Henrietta, or something else? It was Dr. Riley, in fact, who had encouraged the sisters to travel during their year off.

"[Travel] may give you a vision of this world that will determine the direction of your life," wrote Dr. Riley to Henrietta.[1]

Finding God's will for your life is an issue people often struggle with. Henrietta did a lot of thinking about God's will on that trip abroad. Maybe the deeper questions she had concerning how God reveals His will were first sown on that trip—questions she would come to answer fully over time. Some years later, while studying the Scripture passage Philippians 2:12-13, Henrietta's heart and mind were gripped by the familiar words: "Work out your own salvation with fear and trembling. For it is God who works in you both to will and to do of his good pleasure."

"Lord," she prayed, "do you mean to tell me that You are in me and are actually working out Your will and Your pleasure, and I do not need to plead with You and struggle before You to have You show me Your will if I am working out my salvation with fear and trembling? You mean that You are already working in me?"

She turned the pages of her Bible back to Romans 12:1-2 and began to study Paul's words: "I beseech you therefore, brethren, by the mercies of God, that ye present your bodies a living sacrifice, holy, acceptable unto God, which is your reasonable service. And be not conformed to this world: but be transformed by the renewing of your mind, that you may prove what is the good, and acceptable, and perfect will of God!"

Like a spiritual chemist, Henrietta began to put thoughts together and ponder the mixture.

She thought, "If we yield ourselves, He wants to reveal His will to us. How does He reveal His will? If we are 'working out our salvation with fear and trembling,' then God is in us, working out His will and His pleasure through the renewing of our minds! To us, the will of God doesn't have to be a vague, mystical uncertainty; He will renew our minds and direct our thoughts. It is as simple as that. If we yield ourselves to Him, He wants to reveal His will to us. Only our holding back will prevent it!"

With that realization, Henrietta concluded that striving to find the Lord's will—always wondering in which direction to turn—is perhaps the wrong emphasis. Rather, God wants us to know His will even more than we want to know it. Knowing God's will is literally a matter of yielding ourselves to Christ and thinking God's thoughts after Him.[2]

Years later, while on another trip, this time to Korea and Formosa, Henrietta ministered to many weary and frustrated missionaries who were shut out of their mission stations in China and trying to find the will of God for their lives at that crucial time. Her message to them on how the Word of God affects our minds when we yield ourselves to Him was well formulated by then. She said:

> Here is our certainty. God is in us, and He is going to work in us to do His will and pleasure; this is the promise. And through what vehicle will He work to reveal His will except through our minds? We do not have to go chasing a will-o'-the-wisp, or strain after something outside ourselves. God is in us, working out His will and we will be transformed by the renewing of our minds that we may prove what is that good and acceptable and perfect will of God.[3]

But during her sabbatical year Henrietta did much waiting on the Lord as she tried to determine how He was directing her future. And while she believed that waiting on the Lord with all of one's heart is of utmost importance, she also came to believe in working while waiting. Later, she became outspoken in her criticism of people who do too much waiting on the Lord without doing any work while waiting.

> The Lord does most of the waiting, waiting for us to get up and get going. How can the Lord stop you if you haven't started? And how can He change your direction if you aren't moving but are just standing still? You can't steer a car that is standing at the curb. Even if you move the steering wheel, nothing happens. Ask any frustrated little boy who is trying to steer his daddy's parked car!

Before you can guide a car, it has to be moving. So only when we're moving can the Lord direct us. He can stop us, or let us go on, or change the course.

The psalmist says, "Thy word is a lamp unto my feet," which means that the Lord will light one step at a time. When you take a flashlight out into the night, you certainly don't say, "I can't see all the way, so I'm not going to start!" Of course not! You take the step that the flashlight reveals, then you have light enough for the next step; you take that step, and the flashlight gives enough light for one more, and one more, and so you get to your [destination].

When I leave my home and start out for church on Sunday morning, I don't stop and pray on every street corner to see whether I should cross the street or not, or whether I should continue or turn back. I go happily and at peace, knowing that it is the Lord's will for me to go to church. When I come to a stoplight, I don't fret and scream and beat my head and wonder what's wrong; I just stop and wait for the light to turn green and on I go. Even as a preacher once said, "The stops of a good man are ordered of the Lord" instead of "The steps of a good man are ordered of the Lord"; if we yield our wills and commit our way unto the Lord, we can have this confidence that the Lord is directing our paths."[4]

First Visit: Hollywood First Presbyterian Church

On their way back from Europe, Henrietta and Margaret visited California before returning to Minnesota. They remembered Dr. MacLennan's invitation to visit if they were ever in Hollywood and attended his church on the corner of Gower and Carlos Streets.

Dr. MacLennan had taken a little country church and was in the process of building it into one of the most influential pulpits anywhere. But the church was still in its visionary stage. The congregation of about 400 members had built a 1,500-seat sanctuary, nowhere near full yet. A midweek program drew another 500. About another 450 students came to Sunday School, but the program was still in its infancy. It was a growing church in an exploding city. What the church needed was someone to help it jump to the next step.

Henrietta and Margaret stayed for several winter months in Hollywood, visiting the church and enjoying the warm weather. Dr. MacLennan invited Henrietta to speak several times, and her talks consistently received good feedback. She didn't realize it until later, but this was her extended job interview. Just before returning to Minnesota, Dr. MacLennan offered Henrietta the position of director of Christian education at the church. Would she accept?

How could she? Henrietta was already scheduled to resume teaching at Central High. All their friends and family were back in Minnesota. Margaret was involved in business there, and the sisters owned their own home. A move cross-country would mean some huge changes. What were they to do? Henrietta and Margaret traveled back to Minnesota, the decision weighing heavily on them. Friends and family members told them they were crazy even to consider such a move. Dr. MacLennan didn't seem to have any doubts. He wrote—he telegraphed—he telephoned! Was this God's leading? Henrietta wondered.

Not wanting to make a mistake, Henrietta returned to Hollywood for another visit to consider the offer again up close. She knew that even though she had been a success in Minneapolis, that didn't mean she would be a success in Hollywood, a fabulous city of make-believe so far removed from anything she had ever known. Shortly after her arrival, she and Dr. MacLennan went to the Pig 'n' Whistle restaurant on Hollywood Boulevard for lunch. As they approached the entrance, the door opened silently before them. It was a new invention: an electric eye. Henrietta had never seen a door open automatically before. She prayed, "This is just what must happen to me, Father. I must not, dare not, open the door to the decision for myself. You must open it for me. If it is Your will that I should come to Hollywood, open the door, reveal Your plan."

As Henrietta and the pastor ate lunch and talked about the possibilities of the work in Hollywood, Henrietta noticed that more and more she was placing herself in the conversation when talking about what was happening at the church. Instead of saying "Perhaps you could do so and so . . ." she was saying, "I believe we need to do this . . ." During that conversation she realized her own door to decision had opened as silently and effortlessly as had that electric-eye door when she entered the restaurant.

She now wanted the job.

But there were two more problems: her teaching contract and the sale of their house. The school contract had been signed, and homes were in a real estate slump and weren't selling. The contract was easily solved, but selling the home appeared to be impossible. Henrietta decided to up the ante. After reading Judges 6:36-40, the story of how Gideon put out a fleece to find out beyond doubt that God leads, Henrietta increased the asking price of their home by $2,000.

The first person to come and see the house dashed through it with his head down, seemingly seeing nothing at all.

"Well, he's certainly not interested," Henrietta said to Margaret as the man walked out the front door.

That same day, the same man—the first person to see the house—bought it.

The man had actually been so interested in the house, and so afraid that someone else would get to the real estate agent before him, that he had rushed through the tour in order to close the deal quickly at the asking price.

God spoke. And the sisters moved to Hollywood.

Begin with Quality

A Sunday School of 6,000 members is not built overnight. In fact, Henrietta never set numeric goals for herself. She began her new work with one principle learned from an unlikely source.

In the early days of Los Angeles, the tiny suburb of Buena Park was filled with orange groves and farms. There were no freeways or skyscrapers anywhere. There was no haze of brown air overhead. Henrietta and Margaret drove south from Hollywood along a two-lane road. They were on a quest. They knew that somewhere in Buena Park was an amazing restaurant that drew customers from miles around. It wasn't easy to find. There were no huge signs. No obvious markers. The restaurant was located in one of the most inaccessible places around. Finally, they saw among the citrus groves a tiny shack with dozens of cars around it. This must be the place. They stopped and went in. The fried chicken was absolutely delicious. The boysenberry pie was delectable. The women had found what they were looking for.

Knott's Berry Farm was in those days just a diner on the edge of a farm that served amazing food. Today Knott's is an extensive amusement park that draws thousands of people each year. Years later, Henrietta spoke about that first visit to Knott's Berry Farm and the principle on which she would base so much of her ministry:

Because everything was so excellent, people came from miles around. That was a lesson to me: I knew that it did not matter where our church was located; if we had something good, people would come across the country to get it. If the product is good, the people will come. From the first moment my feet entered the First Presbyterian Church of Hollywood, I never tried to build a bigger Sunday School. My only concern was quality. Size came as a result.

Be sure the core of your work is good, or as numbers increase it will collapse. It is never a question of building a bigger Sunday School but rather of building a better one. As a better one is built, more will be attracted to it. Many leaders are anxious to get numbers without planning on what to do with them after they get there! Why attract thousands to a program if you don't have the organization to take care of them?[5]

Quality. That's where she began. Her commitment to quality would catch some off guard. During the very first weeks of her arrival, there was a rush to get out mimeographed announcements for a special meeting. Several people from the college department stayed up nearly all night getting the job done. In triumph they brought the finished product to Henrietta, who took one look and dropped the whole batch of cards in the wastebasket.

"Miss Mears, what do you mean?" they cried. "Look how hard we worked!"

"But look how poorly the job has been done," said Henrietta. "I would rather they didn't go out at all. People will think that is the standard for all our work. We must be Christ-honoring in all that we do."

Her aim was to build a Sunday School that would be as scientifically sound in administration as the finest school system. In Minnesota, Henrietta had been a successful teacher; but now as a director of education in Hollywood, she would have to organize and train others to teach. The first need for the framework of this Sunday School was to have a trained organization of teachers and officers. Henrietta made thorough preparation before she tried to attract children on Sunday. Shortly after arriving on the job, she mapped out the course she was to take. She knew that God's Word was the only infallible guide.

But how would she impart that vision at the very beginning? How would she bring her team up to speed?

The first Tuesday night of each month was set aside for the teachers' meeting. When Henrietta walked into the first meeting, she sensed a frigidity, a reserve, a sitting-back attitude, as if those attending were saying, "We'll have to set aside everything we've done, the way we're doing things, change everything and do everything she wants." A few teachers had already resigned.

"I don't blame them," were Henrietta's thoughts. "I know just how they feel. They've probably had a steady stream of people trying to change them."

After she was introduced, the audience of teachers settled back, arms folded, watchful. But she gave them no flag waving. No call to arms. No passionate appeal to leap up and follow her. Instead, she looked over the edge of her glasses, smiled at them and lowered her voice, almost as if they were fellow conspirators.

"I believe I know just what you're thinking," she said. "You're thinking, 'Here's somebody else to tell us what to do. If I have to reorganize my class once more, or try out some fancy new theory, I'll just die. What does she know about Hollywood, anyway?'"

The group laughed. The ice began to melt.

"You don't like changes, and neither do I," she said. "You've been getting along without me up to now and it would certainly be a great burden on me to have the responsibility of rushing in here and having to try to reorganize everything overnight. So here is my plan. We'll all relax for six months and use the time for observation. Then we'll sit down and evaluate the situation and decide together what we want to do. You'll undoubtedly have some ideas, and I might just possibly have one or two myself."

She smiled and sat down.

Meeting over.

The effect was immediate. The teachers received exactly what they wanted, only now they didn't want it!

No changes for six months?!

Sunday School teachers began rushing up to her. "I can't wait six months. My department is dying for attention. Don't you think we can get started right now?"

Six weeks later, the entire Sunday School felt rejuvenated. A new sense of expectancy and importance filled the ministry. Being a Sunday School teacher suddenly felt like an honor, a privilege, a responsibility. Some who had handed in their resignations changed their minds. The consistent theme was: "We don't want to miss the fun. This is amazing. It's the first time we've seen anything like this."

The Work Begins

If Henrietta's work had been a one-woman program, it would have failed. She was the inspirer, the organizer, the facilitator, the captain. But it was the work of the volunteers that moved the ship forward.

After that first Sunday School meeting, changes began immediately. Henrietta's instructions were that nothing could look old, shabby or unkempt. Sunday School rooms were painted light, fresh colors. Flowers were placed everywhere. Music started to flourish. A junior choir was started. A choir was formed in the college department. Helen Bustard, a close friend of Henrietta's from

Northern California, came down to assist in the music of the church. She had trained in Europe, making her debut in opera in Milan, Italy, and she started many musical groups and organized large spring festivals of music for the church. Henrietta organized what she called "Creative Club," comprising musicians, singers, actors and writers who met monthly in her home for the next 20 years. The college department took off with a bang. The Young Women's Auxiliary began to grow. Prayer and prayer meetings were constant within every group, for every need, for every problem.

Henrietta particularly worked hard to change the perception of teaching Sunday School as women's work. She recruited male leaders in the Sunday School to take positions of authority, knowing that with outstanding men in charge of departments— builders, teachers, lawyers—boys would have an example and girls would keep pace with the boys.

✗ The Dream Gets Underway

Those first few months were a flurry of activity. When Henrietta first surveyed the challenge of building a Sunday School and directing the Christian education program in the Hollywood First Presbyterian Church, she wrote down all the aims and desires she had for the work, all the hopes and dreams that were in her mind and heart.

It was a long list.

It is difficult today to fully grasp just how revolutionary were Henrietta Mears's ideas. Her vision for Christian education was a sea change from the average Sunday School class of her day, in which someone would take all the kids of the church into a back room to tell them a story. If some were too little to get it, they could suck their thumbs; and if some were too old—well, tough! They had to be there because their dad said so.

Henrietta envisioned and created a complete educational ministry, not just a part-time program. She wanted a department for every age group and a class for each specific year of age "from the cradle to the grave"; training for teachers that was of the same caliber as that provided in public schools; a complete curriculum with a growing challenge for each age; a group from the Sunday School that would be called to dedicate themselves to vocational Christian service; clubs for all ages and separate clubs for boys and girls from junior age through high school; a summer camp conference program that would teach youths and give them Christian training; a social life in the church that would be fun-filled and Christ-centered; an atmosphere where people could make Christian friends and where businessmen could meet Christian associates. She wanted to present a missionary vision to each age level; she wanted a student-oriented budget program so that young people would learn stewardship and have a sense of personal contribution to the church and throughout the world. She wanted a Sunday School with appeal for adults and young married couples, so that Christian homes would be established and a spiritual environment developed to nurture children in becoming those who loved the Lord and obeyed His Word. She wanted the appeal of Sunday School to go on beyond elementary age. She wanted a program that would meet the particular need of the hour in terms of the specific demands of each age group, and more.

Impossible?

Not with prayer and a lot of hard work.

The dream gathered steam. In two years, the Sunday School at Hollywood First Presbyterian grew from about 450 people to more than 4,000. A few years later, attendance peaked at 6,000. It wasn't always easy, and Henrietta didn't always make the right decisions. She had been in Hollywood just three years, with the pressure of her work continually mounting when, one day in early summer, she reached a point of near exhaustion. She put her head on her desk and wept.

"It's impossible," she said. "Nobody can do it!"

Her secretary, Ethel May, grabbed her by the arm and rushed her up to Dr. MacLennan's office. He was out, but Henrietta sat in his study for a while, reading Scripture, waiting. She found the verse "As thy days, so shall thy strength be" (Deut. 33:25).

Sitting in the quiet study, she realized the great truth that the Lord will never ask you to do more than you are able to do. She learned to tend to the task that the Lord had given for the day, trusting Him to give the needed strength, but knowing that if tomorrow's task is heaped on today's challenges, it will fail.

That was the Word she needed. She would continue on in this amazing calling. Tomorrow would offer a new set of challenges; but for right now, there was only today.

And God.

And that was enough.

Henrietta Mears

Henrietta Mears at about age 38, when she joined the Hollywood First Presbyterian Church as director of Christian education in 1928.

Age 12 years, 10 months, in August 1903.

Graduation from the University of Minnesota, June 12, 1913.

Henrietta Mears,
"a teacher in
Christ's College."

Henrietta in the last
years of her life.

Teacher entertains a group of collegians with her hilarious "sermon" on "Old Mother Hubbard" from the Book of Numbers—the telephone book.

Teacher tackles a healthy hunk of watermelon at a feed put on by her collegians.

Henrietta traveled not just as a tourist but as one seeking to gain a better perspective of other peoples and take that knowledge back to her young people.

Here in Egypt, at the pyramids, she takes a donkey ride.

And here, Henrietta (L.) and Ethel May continue their tour of the pyramids from a lofty perspective.

At a reception held in honor of Henrietta Mears and her sister Margaret (far right), collegians welcome the two travelers home from their 1947 trip to South America and to war-ravaged Europe.

This 1937 photo was the first taken of young seminarians who grew up in teacher's college department at Hollywood First Presbyterian church. L. to R. (*front row*) are Bob Ferguson, Homer Goddard, Kenneth Cook, Henrietta Mears, Pastor Stuart P. MacLennan, Cyrus Nelson, Bill Dunlap and Kenneth Nelson; (*back row*) Don Cole, Dick Halverson, Ed Rogers, Paul Fisk, Charles Miller, David Cowie and Jack Barnhart. Teacher described her seminarians as "a noble army of men who follow in His train."

A number of Hollywood personalities took part in *Decision*, a film made of Forest Home. At the premiere of *Decision* were several members of the Hollywood Christian Group: (*L. to R., front row*), Connie Haines, Eva Pearson, Colleen Townsend, Lois Chartrand and Henrietta Mears; (*back row*), Bob Mitchell, Charles Turner, Bill Beal, Louis Evans, Jr., L. David Cowie and Murray Bernard.

Dr. J. B. Phillips, translator of The New Testament in Modern English, was among the many outstanding Christian leaders invited by Henrietta Mears to minister at Forest Home. A guest speaker at the 1954 College Briefing Conference, he appears here at Henrietta's immediate left. In this photo are L. to R. (*front row*) Cy Nelson and Bill Dunlap; (*back row*) Bill Bright, Dr. Bob Smith, Dr. Mears, Dr. Phillips and Dale Bruner.

Henrietta Mears, Donn Moomaw and Billy Graham enjoy a reunion and a time of fellowship at a Forest Home banquet.

The first Gospel Light Bible lessons were born in the mind of Henrietta Mears. For some time, she and Ethel May Baldwin were the sole staff.

A shipment of books for a new 1950 curriculum course has just arrived in the Gospel Light warehouse. Looking over one of the first copies are (L. to R.) William T. Greig Jr., William T. Greig Sr., and Cyrus N. Nelson (Cyrus Nelson was president at the time; both William Greig Sr., and William Greig Jr., would become president of Gospel Light in the years to come).

The first warehouse and distribution center for Gospel Light Publications (then Gospel Light Press) was this garage behind the Hollywood home of D. Stanley Engle, one of Henrietta Mears's Sunday School teachers. The Engle dining room became the first Gospel Light office.

The Gospel Light warehouse today in Cincinnati, Ohio.

Henrietta Mears speaks to guests at a celebration in 1958 in recognition of her sixty-eighth birthday and the twenty-fifth anniversary of Gospel Light Publications.

Henrietta Mears blows out the candles on the birthday cake honoring both these events.

(Random quotes about her life and work, taken from
a church bulletin of a tribute service for Miss Mears,
April 21, 1961, two years before her death.)

"Dr. Henrietta C. Mears is one of the greatest Christians I have ever known! I doubt if any other woman outside of my wife and mother has had such a marked influence on my life. Her gracious spirit, her devotional life, her steadfastness for the simple Gospel, and her knowledge of the Bible have been a continual inspiration and amazement to me."

—Rev. Billy Graham

[In 1961, Billy Graham had been working as an evangelist for 14 years and was already recognized worldwide. He would go on to five more decades of international ministry, even gaining entry into closed countries such as the (former) U.S.S.R., China and North Korea. He retired in 2005, passing the reins to his son, Franklin Graham. It is estimated that Billy Graham preached to more than 210 million people in 185 countries.]

"I think Miss Mears has the greatest capacity for loving people of almost anyone I know. She taught me a wonderful lesson. Hollywood Christian Group—Miss Mears and I sitting together

. . . one of the actresses was called upon for her testimony. I sat like the Chief of Pharisees, but Miss Mears was muttering, 'Bless her heart! I just love that girl! She is the dearest thing!' Some of us talk about love. Miss Mears loves."

—Ruth Bell Graham

[The wife of Billy Graham, Ruth Bell Graham also continued ministering for decades after this time. In 1966, she founded the Ruth and Billy Graham Children's Health Center in Asheville, North Carolina. Today she is the mother of 5 children, grandmother of 19, and great-grandmother to a growing number, as well as the author of many books, including Footprints of a Pilgrim, One Wintry Night, *and* Mothers.*]*

"From the time I heard you challenge us to go home and follow the apostle Paul's action in kneeling to ask of God 'What wilt Thou have me to do?' my life began to change. Through your teaching I was encouraged to give my life to Christ and at all costs follow His leading. The establishment of Campus Crusade for Christ has been the result."

—Bill Bright

[When this quote was written, Bill Bright had already founded and had led Campus Crusade for Christ for 10 years. At that time it was present on 40 campuses in the United States and in 2 other countries. Today, as the world's largest Christian ministry, Campus Crusade for Christ serves people in 191 countries through a staff of 26,000 full-time employees and more than 225,000 trained volunteers working in some 60 niche ministries and projects ranging from military ministry to inner-city ministry. Bill Bright wrote The Four Spiritual Laws—*likely the most widely distributed religious booklet in history, with approximately 2.5 billion printed to date. He died in 2003 at age 81.]*

"In a very real sense Miss Mears is responsible for my family. Not only had she been counselor to Doris and me through the years, but she introduced us in her office. I understand that she predicted the introductions would turn out the way it did. There is not an area of my life that her influence has not touched with great significance. Philippians 1:3 expresses my sentiments perfectly concerning her."

—Richard Halverson

[Richard Halverson pursued a career in entertainment in Hollywood in the 1930s before entering the pastoral ministry and being ordained. He first worked as managing director of Forest Home and then at several churches. In 1961, when this quote was written, he was senior pastor of Fourth Presbyterian Church in Washington, D.C. Richard Halverson served as chaplain to the U.S. Senate from 1981-1995 and was a prolific author with such works as Gospel for the Whole of Life, The Word of a Gentleman, The Timelessness of Jesus Christ, Walk with God Between Sundays, Prayers Offered by the Chaplain of the U.S. Senate, We the People, *and many more. An original member of the Fellowship of the Burning Heart, Mr. Halverson, along with Vonette Bright, was influential in having the Senate declare the National Day of Prayer. He died in 1995.]*

"You were my teacher long before you ever heard of me. When I began my work among young people in 1933 I read everything you wrote and listened to everyone who could tell me about you. I tried my best to do things the way you would want them done."

—Jim Rayburn

[Jim Rayburn worked as a Presbyterian youth minister before founding in 1941 the youth outreach organization called Young Life. Today, Young Life ministers to more than 700,000 students annually. Jim Rayburn died in 1970 at age 61.]

"The best thing I ever did for Hollywood Presbyterian church was to get Miss Mears as Director of Christian Education."

—Dr. Stewart MacLennan

[Dr. Stewart P. MacLennan was pastor of Hollywood First Presbyterian Church from 1921 to 1941. During the 13 years of their joint ministry, he and Henrietta Mears worked together in what many people categorized as a dynamic spiritual partnership. Dr. Mac, as he was known, allowed Henrietta full scope in the complete fulfillment of her plans and projects.]

"One thing that will always stand out in my memory about Dr. Mears is her indefatigable and tireless optimism about the Lord and what He can do. Amid all the years of fierce pace and work and occupation, I have never once heard her say she was tired or weary or discouraged, never once did she seem to be sorry for herself but always enthusiastic about what Christ was doing and could do in human lives that were all around."

—Dr. Louis Evans, Sr.

[Dr. Louis Evans, Sr., was pastor of Hollywood First Presbyterian Church from 1941 to 1953, and pastor of National Presbyterian Church from 1973 until 1991. He served Communion to Richard Nixon and his staff and also spent time with Ronald Reagan. Reagan attended National Presbyterian until his assassination attempt. Evans was then asked to visit with the president and serve Communion at the White House on several occasions.]

"How much we love and admire you as a Christian and as a friend."

—Roy Rogers and Dale Evans

[Roy Rogers was a Western film and TV star. In 1948, an estimated 80 million people went to see his films. He made 87 Westerns from 1943 to 1954 and was ranked by theater operators as the No. 1 Western box-office star during those years. He died in 1998, at age 86. His wife, Dale Evans, starred with Rogers in most of her 38 motion pictures and 2 television series. Dale Evans wrote 25 songs, including the couple's theme song, "Happy Trails." After her conversion, Dale became a popular speaker and tireless volunteer with Christian groups. Her 17 books dealt primarily with faith. She died in 2001 at age 88. Before their deaths, the couple founded the Happy Trails Children's Foundation for severely abused children.]

"Teacher is a hard taskmaster. She expects everything for Christ. She has the knack of making you feel that you are the most important person in the whole world. No matter how much she has to do she makes you feel that she has all the time in the world for you. She puts you on your mettle to produce. You had to do it and she wanted you to be able to do it, to feel the sole responsibility, and not to have any feeling that she would do it for you. She literally forced me into being a leader. She pushed me into responsibility."

—Rev. David Cowie

[David L. Cowie started out as a member of the college department at Hollywood First Presbyterian Church and was challenged by Henrietta Mears to go into pastoral ministry. He served in several churches including as senior pastor of Seattle's University Presbyterian Church from 1948 to 1961.]

"Long before it was my privilege to meet you personally, I had learned to be thankful for the great work that you are doing.

Not only has yours been a mission to young people but to adults as well, and only eternity will reveal the far-reaching effect of your devotion to the cause of Christ and making his love known around the world."

—Gov. Mark Hatfield

[After two terms in the Oregon State House of Representatives and two years in the Oregon State Senate, Mark Hatfield became the youngest secretary of state in Oregon history in 1956 at age 34. Two years later, he was elected governor of Oregon, and became the state's first two-term governor in the twentieth century when he was re-elected in 1962. In 1966, Hatfield won a seat in the U.S. Senate, a position he retained for five terms. Senator Hatfield retired in 1996, having never lost an election. After retiring, he joined the faculty of George Fox University. As of 2006, he is Emeritus Distinguished Professor of Politics.]

"It was summer and some of those interested in organizing the Hollywood Christian Group suggested the plan be set aside until fall. 'Then forget about it!' commanded Teacher adamantly. 'If it's worth doing in the fall, it's worth doing now, but if you wait until fall all the sparkle and enthusiasm will be gone . . . like a lukewarm glass of ginger ale with all the fizz gone. What is the first night you can get started?' Three nights later the first meeting was held in her home in Westwood. Teacher's influence has been felt by this group from the beginning."

—Connie Haines

[By 1961, when this quote was written, Connie Haines had already had a remarkable career as a Hollywood entertainer—both as a singer and as an actress. She appeared in six movies in the 1940s and had a memorable career as a big-band singer with Harry James. Connie landed the vocal spot on the Abbott

& Costello radio show and continued with them for four years. During World War II she appeared on many of the radio shows produced for the armed forces overseas. She guest-starred on the Bing Crosby, Bob Hope, Jack Benny, and George Burns radio shows, and on the "Command Performance" show with Clark Gable and Betty Grable. Throughout her singing career, she made over 200 recordings, appearing with Frank Sinatra, Smokey Robinson, Tommy Dorsey, and more. Unique in the history of entertainment, Connie appeared in "Command Performances" at The White House for five U. S. Presidents: Eisenhower, Johnson, Kennedy, Reagan and Bush Sr. In 1988, President Ronald Reagan presented Connie with the "Courage Award of 1988" for her courage in overcoming cancer. She is a National Spokesperson for the American Cancer Society today.]

"If I were to single out a dominant impression of Miss Mears, in addition to those perhaps most obvious: indefatigable energy, her absorbing interest in individuals, her lust for life (symbolized significantly by her hats), it would be her all-consuming passion for excellency. Whether by requesting a coat and tie for dinner, or by meticulous planning for a meeting, or infinite preparation for a lesson, or the use of time, Miss Mears always demanded of herself and enjoyed in others, excellence."

—Dale Bruner

[Dr. Dale Bruner came to know Christ at Hollywood First Presbyterian Church. He earned his M.Div. at Princeton Theological Seminary and his Ph.D. at Germany's Hamburg University. After teaching for 11 years at Union Theological Seminary in the Philippines, he went to Whitworth College in 1975. During his years as George & Lyda Wasson Professor of Religion at Whitworth, Dr. Bruner touched the lives of countless students. He became one

of Whitworth's most influential professors and his influence extended far beyond the generation of students he taught and mentored. During his tenure at the college, he authored several books and spoke and taught at hundreds of churches all over the country. He became one of the most sought-after speakers in the Presbyterian Church. Since his retirement in 1997, he continues to have a vital teaching ministry in the PCUSA.]

"Both brother Don, who soon gets his second doctorate from London University, and I are in the ministry because of the manner in which you allowed the Holy Spirit to use your life in our midst."

—Dr. Edward Cole

[When Dr. Edward Cole said this, he was pastor at First Baptist Church, Pomona, California.]

"The many times of prayer with you through the years, in many places and for many purposes, are among my fondest memories because they brought me so close to our Lord."

—Dr. Bob Munger

[At the time, Dr. Bob Munger was pastor of First Presbyterian Church, Berkeley, California. He later became an author and a professor at Fuller Seminary.]

"The priceless memories of the high points of my life are inextricably interwoven with thoughts of you. There was the influence of your life on mine: at a crucial time of decision, in your lovely home, at Forest Home. I saw in your life the reality of Christ, the vitality of faith, the consistency of daily living. The inspiration of your life lives with us through the years and even touches our children's lives."

—Edie Munger

[Edie Munger is Dr. Bob Munger's wife and ministry partner.]

"Her ardent zeal for missions, both home and abroad, communicated to youth with her unique eloquence, has probably enlisted more men and women for Christ's service than any other woman's voice in the history of our church."

—Donn Moomaw

[Donn Moomaw was a professional football player who later became a pastor. He read the prayers at both of President Ronald Reagan's inaugurations.]

"What a work you have done. There is no young people's or Sunday School work in this nation which is equal to what you have accomplished. When I think of the tens of thousands of young people who have studied the Bible under your leadership, of the thousands of young people who have faced the claims of Christ and made commitments to Him, of the scores of young men who have gone into the ministry and other young people into Christian service, I cannot but stand back in amazement. Somehow I feel that you were made for California. Whenever I think of you I think of the biggest: the biggest youth conference. The biggest young people's work, the biggest Sunday School, the biggest Sunday School publishing house. Your vision has encompassed the world, and God has privileged you to see the fruit of your labors."

—Dr. Harold Ockenga

[Dr. Harold Ockenga was a leading figure of twentieth-century American evangelicalism. He served for many years as pastor of Park Street Congregational Church in Boston, Massachusetts. He was also a prolific author on biblical, theological, and devotional topics. Dr. Ockenga helped found the Fuller Theological Seminary and Gordon-Conwell Theological Seminary, as well as the National Association of Evangelicals. He died in 1985.]

CHAPTER 5

Branching Out

*Our message is the Word of God. Our field is the
minds of people. Our tools are paper and ink.*

—HENRIETTA MEARS

Sometimes our greatest works come not as a goal we set
out to achieve but as a result of filling a need along the
way. This was the way it was with Sunday School curriculum.
Henrietta Mears never set a goal other than creating better lessons.
A greater work than she could have imagined branched out from
that goal.

Her primary focus was always on Sunday School—and her
Sunday School grew. It grew and grew and grew. Henrietta Mears
was continually energized by a vision to see people come to Christ,
specifically through the vehicle of Sunday School. For her it was a
life calling that meant unswerving dedication, perseverance and
resolve. The temptation in Hollywood was to create programs
based on sensationalism and the obvious Hollywood attractions.
But Henrietta always aimed to create ministries based on "earnest
prayer, solid theology and an environment of love, warmth and
enthusiasm where people found answers to their life problems."
She pulled no punches when describing the secret of her success:
it came through prayer. Her success also came from nose-to-the-
grindstone work. She wrote:

I have had so many people say to me, "Oh Miss Mears, I wish I could do all the things you do. Why, I would give anything if I could have the results you have in your Sunday School!"

Well, let me tell you right now that I don't believe you! You watch the organist play so beautifully at your church, and you say, "I would give anything to be able to play as she does!"

But your mother and father spent hundreds of dollars on your music lessons when you were a child, and you were too busy to practice. Instead, you went out to play with your friends.

So it is with your Sunday School class: you don't have results because you don't take the time or make the effort to do anything about your teaching to learn more about your students. I tell you truthfully that I have never seen a teacher who was willing to invest time and effort in his class who was not successful—that is, if he was teaching the right age class.[1]

A Surprising Direction

Henrietta knew that one important component to her Sunday School would be quality curriculum. Curriculum enabled teachers to teach solid material in a creative manner over long periods of time—sometimes over a period of years.

To put this in perspective, a pastor typically invests at least one complete workday per week (at least 8 to 10 hours, sometimes twice that) to prepare a 30-minute sermon. A pastor is also trained (sometimes for four to eight years in college and graduate school) to study the Scriptures to draw out correct interpretations and applications. A pastor will often study public speaking techniques, attend seminars and read books about teaching, preaching and connecting with audiences, and have his intuition finely honed when seeking creative illustrations to help keep lessons interesting.

It is almost impossible for a Sunday School volunteer, who doesn't have the resources, the training or the time to prepare a solid Bible study from scratch week after week, year after year, to be effective at it. Good curriculum provides a healthy, sustainable, visionary Christian education ministry. It prevents burnout, enables consistent creativity and ensures theological consistency and depth.

Good curriculum can make or break a ministry.

One of the first things Henrietta asked her boss, Dr. MacLennan, upon arrival was if he had a preference for materials used in Sunday School.

"Use anything you want as long as it teaches the Bible," Dr. MacLennan said.

Henrietta had been on the curriculum committee for the Minneapolis public school district and knew how important good curriculum was. She requested and received sample curricula from several Sunday School publishing houses. Then she gathered the educators of the church together to survey the available curriculum. Most of the materials were biblically sound, but all seemed inadequate in one way or another. Many lessons were just bland—there were no pictures, no activities, and the wording was not geared toward children. Most lessons were not graded for any particular age. None presented material chronologically, which Henrietta believed would lead to confusion. For example, on one Sunday, a student would study an Old Testament lesson about Saul the king; the next Sunday he might study a New Testament lesson about Saul of Tarsus. "Are we talking about the same Saul here?" students would invariably ask. Henrietta termed this "the grasshopper method" of Bible study. In the most widely used curriculum, the story of Creation was presented only once in a span of several years. If a child missed that Sunday, he or she would have to find out somewhere other than in Sunday School how the world began.

After a familiar curriculum supply ran out, Henrietta seized the opportunity to head in a new direction—she would write the church's own material.

It was a huge task. Henrietta sat down with the educators in the church and worked out a prospectus, determining the accomplishments expected at each age level. Then she began studying and writing. She recruited Esther Ellinghusen to help prepare lessons. Esther was a teacher in the Los Angeles public school system as well as superintendent of the church's junior department. Before beginning to write, the women interviewed other teaching specialists, studied vocabulary charts and compared school textbooks for size of type, vocabulary, sentence structure and illustrations. Word puzzles, mazes and crossword puzzles were added to boost creativity and increase student interest.

These were the days before laptops, copiers and desktop publishing. So Henrietta's secretary, Ethel May, took the written pages, typed them up on wax-backed tablets to copy them on a mimeograph machine, and then stapled them into books. Another ultra-modern machine—a *multigraph*—was purchased so that titles on book covers could be handset and printed with fancier fonts. The team collected calendars and cut out the pictures to paste on the covers. These first homemade books may have looked crude by today's standards, but they were way ahead of anything else available then.

As the need grew for increased quantities of the lesson books, Henrietta inquired about having them professionally printed and was told that the cost of doing so was completely out of reach. Ethel May recruited her parents to help copy and staple books. The publishing team grew to five.

By 1931, with several years' worth of the church's own curriculum under their students' belts, there was a noticeable change in the Sunday School department at Hollywood First Presbyterian Church. Parents began driving their children to Hollywood from neighboring towns, some from a distance of 50 miles—in a time when there were no freeways! Visitors began to comment on how much Bible students knew. Kids were able to answer questions intelligently, enthusiastically and with understanding.

"If the Bible is taught the way it should be, it will be like a powerful magnet drawing children and youth unto the Lord Jesus Christ," Henrietta said.

"What lesson material are you using, Miss Mears?" visitors would invariably ask.

"Oh, just some mimeographed material that some of us are writing and putting together here," Henrietta would answer, with a tip of the head and slight shrug of her shoulders.

"Is their any way we could get these lessons?"

"Such a thing would be out of the question," Henrietta would say. "We are hardly able to produce it fast enough for our own use."

But word continued to get out, and requests to use her material continued to come in, first at a trickle, and then at a torrential rate.

Agents of Change

It took one persistent person to change Henrietta's mind.

Henrietta's Sunday School lessons were revolutionary. There simply was nothing else like them available. She based the lessons entirely on Scripture, with fresh, relevant, applicable illustrations. The lessons were Christ-centered and each lesson was tailored to fit individual age groups: written in the language of the kinder-garten or primary age child, and in such a way to capture the junior mind, challenge a junior high student, win the high school young person and earn the full approval of the college student. Material was not purposely divisive or controversial. The Bible had promised milk for babies, bread for youth and meat for adults, and Henrietta based her lessons on the appropriate material and Scripture for all those ages.

About her intent in writing lessons, Henrietta wrote:

> It is a terrifying spiritual condition to see elders and dea-cons in churches having to be put in spiritual high chairs with bibs around their necks and fed spiritual milk. Yet that is what will happen if our children do not learn Scripture and Bible truths while they are young. Youth must not be strangled with spiritual truths far beyond their comprehension; the material must be graded and have logical progression through God's Word.[2]

Others saw how beneficial Henrietta's lessons were and wanted them.

Henrietta always said no.

Too busy.

Sorry.

Mr. Marion Falconer, a pharmacist in Anaheim, California, and Sunday School superintendent of another Presbyterian church in that area, invited Henrietta to speak to his teachers on Christian education techniques, and then toured Henrietta's department.

A few months after their first meeting, Mr. Falconer visited Hollywood First Presbyterian again, but this time, he had a deter-mined look in his eye.

"Miss Mears," he said, "I have been asking you repeatedly for copies of your Sunday School literature. I must have copies of your lessons."

Persistent and persuasive, Mr. Falconer presented Henrietta with strong reasons why her lessons should be printed.

Finally he said, "Miss Mears, I will not leave this church until you give me some copies of the material or until I have your promise that it will be printed."

Something in the earnestness of his plea struck a responsive chord in Henrietta. She changed her response from what had always been a definite no and promised she would look into the matter again.

Years later, Henrietta credited Marion Falconer as being the catalyst for change and, inadvertently, beginning a publishing company.

"He just wouldn't take no for an answer," she said.

Henrietta began to brainstorm ways of cutting printing costs. She contacted Harry Rimmer, an old friend from Minnesota, who was now a scientist and lecturer at Hollywood First Presbyterian. He frequently printed paper-covered books of his lectures. Harry put Henrietta in touch with his printer, Cary Griffin, in nearby Glendale. Cary, a believer, caught the vision almost immediately. Their motivation wasn't profit—it was the opportunity to influence. The curriculum just needed to get out there. Could enough books be sold to recoup expenses?

Cary agreed to hold his invoicing, except when he had to make a cash layout, as for engravings. Then he would have to have money up front. He also would help design pages. An accountant with the Union Oil Company, Stanley Engle, volunteered to handle the shipping, distribution and accounting operations. A first printing of 1,000 copies of a junior lesson book was shipped to Henrietta's office. Nobody had realized how much space 1,000 books would take. Boxes were everywhere.

"Next time we'll put them in my garage," Stanley offered.

And so, Stanley Engle's single-car garage became the first warehouse and distribution center of a new Sunday School curriculum publishing company. The Engles' dining room became the first business office. The engravings of that first junior book cost $84.74.

"Well, that's money down the drain," said Stanley's mother.

The new company was named Gospel Light Press. It had no start-up capital, no rented facilities and no full-time employees. Its straightforward aim: "To teach the Word clearly and correctly to the end that people may come to know Christ as Savior and Lord and to grow spiritually, faithful in every good work."

Would the start-up publishing company ever succeed?

In 1933, Gospel Light Press obtained its first copyright. Other writers were added; twelve full courses of curriculum were published before year's end, officially launching Gospel Light Press as the first Sunday School publisher to provide age-graded Bible lessons.

The feedback on the curriculum was immediate and positive. Stories poured in of students and teachers digging into the material. Mothers told of finding their sons on their knees in prayer, doing what was presented in the lessons. To Henrietta, these responses were evidence of God's seal on the books. Orders soon came in to the Engle dining room from churches across the country. By the end of 1933, a total of 13,366 books had been sold to 131 Sunday Schools in 25 states. Through the end of 1934, sales tripled and more books were added. A line of colorful new visual aids, called flannelgraphs, were introduced. (A flannelgraph was a flannel-covered board that sat on an easel, with cut-out figures of people, animals and objects that could be stuck to the flannel to illustrate the lesson as the teacher told a story.) The Engle home became an annex to their garage-warehouse. Books were piled high in corners and under tables. Stanley's wife took telephone orders and processed mail throughout the day. In the evenings, Stanley worked on the accounting records, tied up bundles of books and shipped them cross-country.

Three years of spectacular growth prompted Gospel Light Press to move operations to a larger location, this time a storefront at 1443 NE Vine Street in Hollywood. It was either that or find a new house for the Engles! On Thanksgiving Day, 1936, the four founding partners—Henrietta Mears, Esther Ellinghusen, Ethel May Baldwin and Stanley Engle—held a thanksgiving service in their new location, two blocks from the flashing lights of the film capital's most famous corner, Hollywood and Vine.

The work went on. To cut shipping costs, Stanley discovered that Campbell's Soup boxes were exactly the right size for shipping Gospel Light books. He scoured area stores looking for used boxes. Sales continued to roll in. Clerks, typists and shippers were added. Esther Ellinghusen took a year's leave of absence from her public school teaching and toured the Pacific Northwest, holding workshops, visiting churches and demonstrating the new Sunday School curricula.

By the end of 1937, more than a quarter of a million books had been sold. The company—and its aim—were well underway.

A Tree Grows in Hollywood

Another surprising outreach began, this time as a branch of the new publishing company.

By 1938, inquiries were pouring in for leadership training courses. Churches had Henrietta Mears's curriculum; now they needed to know how to use it correctly to teach their classes. In response, Henrietta joined with several others in launching a

Christian Education Training Course. The first seminar was held at Clifton's Cafeteria in downtown Los Angeles. Henrietta reserved space for 200 people.

More than 500 people showed up. When Henrietta arrived, she could hardly make her way through the crowd. Sunday School teachers from all over the city had shown up, wanting to learn how they could more effectively teach God's Word. These classes were held for several years in a series of Monday night workshops.

Over time, the classes developed into conferences, rallies and conventions across North America. Henrietta became a cofounder of the National Sunday School Association, and she spoke to tens of thousands at conventions in America and Canada.

By the time World War II ended in 1945, Gospel Light Press was one of the four largest independent publishers of Sunday School literature in America. All across the country, youth were being taught that God loved them and had a plan for their lives. Through the training conferences, men and women who thought they could never teach Sunday School were now being trained and equipped. Attendance at Sunday Schools across the country multiplied far beyond expectations.

It was the start of a movement that began in a wood garage in California. Today, Gospel Light is a worldwide Bible curriculum and book publishing company that creates and distributes a wide range of curriculum for children and adults, as well as books and DVDs for the faith-based marketplace.

The company also has a trade book division, Regal, that publishes a wide variety of books geared to the Church and to cultural renewal, covering a wide range of ages, and categories such as personal and spiritual growth, worship, church leadership, business and the workplace, current issues, family and relationships.

Gospel Light's West Coast office, located in Ventura, California, houses some 150 employees. With more than 200 publishing partners, the nonprofit portion of the company, Gospel Light Worldwide, licenses rights to print its books and curriculum in more than 50 languages for distribution in 48 countries. Some of the countries with special curriculum projects include Armenia, Albania, Bosnia, China, Egypt, Georgia, Lebanon, Poland, Romania, Russia and South Africa. Hundreds of thousands of children and adults worldwide have been impacted by the Bible curriculum developed through the ministry of Gospel Light.

Henrietta wrote:

Does not God want us to be concerned with the youth of our age? What am I to do about taking the Gospel to them? I must stand at attention before the Lord of Israel. I can hear Him speaking to me, as He did to Moses: God, deliver my people. What does God want you to do? Meet with Him face-to-face, and you will find out.[3]

CHAPTER 6

Faith-Sized Goals

Faith is the substance of things hoped for,
the evidence of things not seen.

HEBREWS 11:1, *NKJV*

Ministry to people is the business of changing lives—but we don't do the changing; God does. He uses us as the hands and feet of Christ. It is He—not us—who ultimately moves in hearts to effect change. Faith, then, needs to be the core of every decision, every move, every assessment, every choice associated with ministry.

And faith leads to strategy.

By prayer, logic and surveying her surroundings and social climate, Henrietta Mears knew that some projects would prove more helpful than others. In that day, (and today as well) Henrietta knew that no church ministry is complete without a solid camping component.

Camping programs are high yield. When it comes to spiritual formation in people's lives, a good camping ministry is a harvest field. Taking people away from their regular life for a few days, for a week, perhaps, or maybe even for a summer, and offering them a season of activity, intense focus without distractions, peer-to-peer interaction and Bible influence is perhaps one of the greatest investments in people's lives. Camp is synonymous with friends and fun, of stillness from the world's pull and of open hearts and spiritual decisions. A week at a good camp can often accomplish spiritually in a student's life what it takes years to do otherwise.

As soon as Henrietta began her job at Hollywood First Presbyterian Church, she began to develop a camping program and to search for a place where she could establish camping grounds. Those early years were filled with challenges and the unexpected.

It would take an incredible amount of faith to see this camping ministry become a reality.

A Pioneer Work

In 1929, Henrietta took 125 college students to Switzer's Camp in the San Bernardino Mountains east of Los Angeles. After the road to the camp ended, students walked the rest of the way—about 4 miles. The first year, Henrietta hiked with them. But after that, someone suggested she might like to ride on a pack mule. She tried it and found it much more to her liking. For the first two years, she was the only adult at the camp and did the cooking as well as the speaking and counseling. Midweek, she always returned to the church for the college prayer meeting then climbed back up the mountain to camp.

Henrietta recalled much success in those first few years of camping, rugged though it was. Students committed their lives to Christ for the first time. Some made commitments to full-time Christian ministry. Others simply progressed in their faith, allowing Christ to affect their hearts and change their lives.

But Switzer's Camp had its limitations. In 1930, Henrietta sent four of her college students to check out a young people's conference at the Mt. Hermon Christian Camping Center, located more than 400 miles away in Northern California. Mt. Hermon had long been established and was well equipped. The students brought back a positive report. The next year, and for several years afterward, Henrietta took her students there.

One of the regular highlights of Mt. Hermon was sponsoring a big parade. Students drove from the campgrounds into nearby Santa Cruz, horns blaring, as the parade wound its way down to the beach where students descended on ice cream shops. One year, Henrietta, Ethel May Baldwin and church secretary Dorothy Drew Choate rode in the parade in a ramshackle taxicab, outrageously made-up and costumed as comic characters.

For many, Mt. Hermon became a place of reflection and retrospection, repentance and renewal. But the 800-mile round-trip became a concern for Henrietta. These were the days before freeways, and the long distance travel kept some students from going to camp.

She needed to find something closer to home.

For a few years, Henrietta took her students to Camp Bethel near San Dimas. Camp Bethel was large enough to hold several age groups at one time. The site was closer to Los Angeles than Mt. Hermon, yet it was far enough away to discourage parents from dropping in for a visit and leaving behind a bunch of homesick kids. It was also far enough away to discourage college students from driving up for a meeting instead of attending an entire conference.

But Camp Bethel was not without its challenges. During summer months, the campsite itself became one large dust bowl. The swimming pool was about the size of a large bathtub. The main auditorium—when not occupied by campers—did double duty as a chicken coop. Most other buildings were flimsy portables on stilts. Why stilts? Henrietta found out during one of the camps.

During a winter conference in 1936, rain began to fall in torrents. Standing water rose. That night, campers in their canvas-sided cabins heard the rush of water under and around their cabins. All was dark outside—visibility nonexistent. That night

Henrietta stayed up, praying that the camp would be spared from serious harm. In the morning, daylight revealed muddy water covering the campsite—most places were about a foot deep—except for a small island of elevated ground where the dining room sat marooned. This one dry place was large enough to hold the entire group of campers. But how would they get there? Henrietta arranged for all the cars in camp to be parked side by side to form a bridge. Campers were able to walk from one car to another without having to wade through the water.

The camp must go on, flood or no flood.

One popular camp speaker was a young scientist named Bud Moon. He was a believer who demonstrated scientific marvels to the students and drew Bible applications from them. During one talk, Bud demonstrated a new kind of machine called a wire recorder. He recorded his voice and then let the students hear the recording. He erased the tape and played it again. This time it didn't make a sound. He reminded his listeners of Matthew 12:36-37 that tells us we are to give an account of every idle word spoken. Years later, Bud Moon became known as Dr. Irwin A. Moon, director of the Moody Institute of Science.

Changed Hearts, Changed Lives

Camp, like all ministry situations, is not about numbers but about changed hearts. Even in the early years, stories of such spiritual change poured forth.

Once, at Bethel, some boys were involved in an argument. As Bill Dunlap, one of the young boys, prepared to go to Henrietta's cabin for discipline, he was warned by his brother, "Watch out, Bill. Don't let Miss Mears pray with you. If you do, you'll be a goner."

Bill and his partner in crime stood before Henrietta, who, if the need arose, added camp disciplinarian to her roster of duties.

Henrietta was aware that most Hollywood youths had a scanty spiritual heritage, if any, and that disciplined behavior was not their most natural attribute. She reminded herself about a colleague who told two boys who turned a church balcony into a racetrack to "get out and stay out!" And that is exactly what those boys did. Did they ever again enter another church? Henrietta doubted it.

"Boys," she said, "we need to pray first about what happened this afternoon. Will you join me please?"

As Bill knelt, he literally held his fists in front of his face, ready to defend himself against prayer. He resolved that when Henrietta began to pray, he was going to run out of the room, leave camp and never come back there or to Sunday School.

A minute passed in silence. Five minutes passed. Then ten. Henrietta remained absolutely silent.

Don, the other culprit, broke the tension.

"Lord," Don prayed, "if there is anything in my life that is keeping the Holy Spirit from blessing this conference, show it to me."

Bill was flabbergasted. His companion in crime had been the first to have a change of heart.

Still Henrietta remained silent.

For the first time, Bill realized he had free choice. He could say no to God if he wanted to, and no one, not even Henrietta Mears, would question his decision.

"God, here is my life," Bill prayed. "Whatever You want. If you want me to be a garbage collector for the honor and glory of Jesus Christ, I'll be one."[1]

Years later, Bill, now grown and an influential pastor who would one day preach the gospel to President Dwight D. Eisenhower, stood before his congregation and retold the incident.

"My life was changed from that moment on," said Pastor Dunlap. "My father was the founder and president of 42 department stores. I was slated to be his heir. If Miss Mears had prayed one word that afternoon, I would have left the camp and would be in the business world today. But she kept still and allowed God to speak to us. I learned then that I was not responsible to her, but to Christ. And that is why I am in pastoral ministry today."

During another camp, a young collegian named Bob Ferguson stood up during a testimony time and told the group he simply couldn't believe in Christ. Bob left camp that night—he literally walked away from the bonfire circle where everyone was gathered— determined to be honest with his doubts while hoping to seek truth. The group was stunned by his actions. Henrietta stood up and began praying for him—thanking the Lord for Bob's complete honesty while asking God to give Bob the clarity he was searching for.

Bob went on to study at the University of Oxford, England. He was a champion debater. Even though he struggled with his faith, he always took the side of faith in any debate. God was working in his life. One summer he bicycled through Europe on a recreational mountain climbing expedition, staying at youth hostels along the way. He didn't have the money to join guided mountain-climbing groups, but he would sometimes trail a group, letting them lead the way for safety. On one such climb of the Matterhorn in the Swiss Alps, Bob followed a group higher and higher up the mountain. He wore only his street clothes and sneakers—having no money for equipment. As the climb progressed, Bob realized he was past the point of no return. It was impossible for him to turn around and go back alone.

Bob continued to climb higher and higher, uncertain what to do other than go forward alone. Finally, Bob reached an impasse: Behind him lay an impossible descent; in front of him was a crevasse too wide to cross by himself. His only hope was to jump for a rope that hung down in the middle of the crevasse. If he reached the rope, he could perhaps gain enough momentum to swing to the other side. It was life or death. He knew he would have to jump; he knew he might not be able to reach the rope; he knew that even if he did reach it, his cold hands might not be able to hold on to the rope. And even if he could hold on, he might not have enough force to swing to the other side.

Bob stood for a long time, watching the sun sink into the night. There, on the ledge, he began to sense the presence of God like never before. He was not alone—not then, not ever. "God," he prayed, "if You help me make this, I'll serve You until I die."

And then he jumped.

On the other side, Bob sobbed with relief, gratitude and new-found faith. He ran along the trail now until he caught up with the guided tour. They were amazed to see a lone hiker so far up, particularly so inadequately equipped, and took him back down to safety.

The next summer at camp, Bob stood up during another testimony time and told the group how he had discovered faith, alone, with nowhere to turn, on the side of a mountain.

Bob left Oxford, where he had a scholarship, to go to Princeton Theological Seminary. He filled out his application so honestly, describing his doubt and newfound belief, that he startled the president, Dr. John Mackay. Dr. Mackay contacted Henrietta for a reference, and Bob was admitted. Bob finished seminary, entered pastoral ministry and later became a Navy chaplain. Years later, when Henrietta took a year's leave of absence from Hollywood First Presbyterian, she left her Sunday School in Bob's care while she was gone.[2]

God's Odds

Henrietta continued to take her students to Camp Bethel, Mt. Hermon and Camp Radford, but she envisioned more. In the summer of 1937, while holding a high school camp at Camp Radford, a phone call came from a friend of Henrietta's, Bill Irwin, whose children went to Sunday School at Hollywood First Presbyterian. Bill knew that Henrietta had been looking for a campsite and encouraged her to take a look at a private estate up in the San Bernardino Mountains called the Forest Home Resort.

Forest Home had been *the* resort in that area for years. Henrietta drove to the site with conference dean Cyrus Nelson. By car, they toured the tree-shaded grounds, the dining room, round house, fish pond and lodge and were overwhelmed by the grandeur of the setting, the magnificent stonework and expensive timbers.

"Don't even bother to stop, Cy," Henrietta said. "Just turn to the left of that round house and go on back down the highway. I know we can't afford all of this." She swept her arm. "This is ridiculous. The buildings alone are far too elaborate for our pocketbooks, and certainly we can't begin to pay for the land."

They turned around, dismissing Forest Home completely from their minds.

But not everyone was convinced the case was closed. Bill Irwin phoned Henrietta to inquire about the trip. He had done some research on the property. Forest Home had been appraised at $350,000—a staggering fortune for anyone in 1937, particularly during the Great Depression. But the seller was motivated to sell. The property's owner was elderly and in poor health, facing major surgery, possibly death. His son did not want to chance the possibility of having to pay the inheritance tax on such a place. Bill was sure that any reasonable offer would be considered—perhaps even an "unreasonable" offer. He convinced Henrietta to offer $50,000 and take out an option to purchase the property—a move that holds the deal until cash can be raised.

"This is a moment for action, not speculation," Henrietta thought, and rounded up people to see the place. Interest in the campsite was instantaneous. Church members, friends and acquaintances drove up to see the grounds, well within driving distance of Los Angeles. Enthusiasm spread as people caught the vision of what could be.

But $50,000, even though it was a rock-bottom offer for the campgrounds still proved an impossible sum to raise. Consider that the salary of the average American worker in 1937 was about $25 a week. Various fund-raising strategies were discussed, but in the end, the decision was made to let the option go.

Forest Home was a "no go."

Have you ever had a dream that didn't end as you planned? You thought God was leading in a particular direction—a good direction—but then, even after several "faith" hurdles had been crossed, the door was still closed? All you could think was, "God, what are You doing? Is this what You want, or are You asking us to believe in You in a way we have never known You before?"

Picture the story of Gideon going out to battle the Midianites in Judges 7. The enemy is huge, powerful—"settled in the valley, thick as locusts. Their camels could no more be counted than the sand on the seashore."

"You have too many men for me to deliver Midian into your hands," God says to Gideon, "in order that Israel may not boast against me that her own strength has saved her."

So 22,000 soldiers are sent home.

"Still too many men," God says. So nearly 10,000 more are sent home.

Finally, a God-sized army emerges: 300 soldiers—impossible odds.

But God says move forward to victory.

That winter a storm ripped through the Forest Home Resort. Three cabins were washed away and a fourth was left hanging over the stream bank. Though much of the surrounding properties lay in complete ruins, the rest of Forest home remained relatively unharmed.

After the storm, Bill Irwin phoned Henrietta. The son of the owner had phoned, offering to sell Forest Home for a new price.

Henrietta prayed. She opened her Bible and turned to Joshua 1:2-3, "Now then, you and all these people, get ready to cross the Jordan River into the land I am about to give to them." Henrietta found her answer in these words. A nonprofit corporation was formed known as Forest Home, Incorporated. The papers were signed.

Forest Home was purchased for $30,000.

A Place of Faith

Henrietta had a definite philosophy about camping that could be summed up in one word: *decision*. If Sunday School was the place where people were built up in the faith, then camp was where they made their decisions about following the Lord. That one word, "decision," permeated every meeting of every camp. Three foundational themes followed—accepting Christ as Savior and Lord, growing in faith, and developing a vision for the world. In the years that followed, thousands of young people made decisions for Christ at Forest Home. Innumerable others decided on life careers in ministry while there.

The early camping ministry at Forest Home proved to be cutting edge in many regards. To begin with, unlike many other camps, Forest Home was purposely nondenominational. Early on, there was some pressure to make it exclusively a Presbyterian camp, but Henrietta believed that would only limit who attended, as well as foster a possessive and exclusive attitude.

The camps were also interracial during a time when many churches weren't as open to multiracial community as they are now. Students came to the camp and mixed together with people from many heritages, including African-American, Japanese,

Chinese and Hispanic. Shortly after World War II ended in 1945, a camp was held at which three former soldiers attended: One had been in the American Air Force and had bombed Germany; another was German and had flown in Hitler's Luftwaffe; the third was Japanese and had flown for his country in the war. None knew that the others were attending. None were Christians. At the camp's final meeting around the campfire, the German soldier stood to accept Christ. The other two were so moved that they stood by him and also accepted Christ. The three stood with arms around each other, tears streaming down their faces, while the entire group sang a classic hymn of fellowship and forgiveness:

Blest be the tie that binds
Our hearts in Christian love;
The fellowship of kindred minds
Is like to that above.[3]

Henrietta put as much work into the selection of conference speakers as she did into everything else and succeeded in getting the very best for the various camps. She brought in outstanding Christian leaders from all over the nation and the world. She often encouraged the speakers to be flexible with their messages, able to shift direction midweek depending on the needs of campers. Volunteer counselors helped the campers apply the speakers' messages to their individual needs. Often when a camp seemed to be going well, Henrietta would call a meeting and drop what came to be known as her "anti-complacency bombs," urging a stronger spiritual focus. Did there need to be more emphasis on the power of the Holy Spirit? What about God's concern for the lost? If testimony times seemed stale, or ideas unimaginative, Henrietta consistently pushed for something more alive.

One of the many young people whose lives were touched at Forest Home was Jim Rayburn. Jim went on to establish his own international youth ministry, Young Life, which in turn spawned Malibu Camps. Today, Young Life programs are active in all 50 states and more than 45 countries, reaching an estimated 1 million teenagers annually. Approximately 120,000 middle school and high school students are involved with Young Life on a weekly basis. More than 75,000 kids spend a weekend during the school year or a week in the summer at one of Young Life's 21 camping properties in the United States and Canada. Jim based much of his camping philosophy on what he learned at Forest Home.

Henrietta Mears continually reached toward the limitless, infinite possibilities of living for God. She wanted to know all the things God has prepared for them who love Him (see 1 Cor. 2:9). Forest Home became a prime example of what God could do through a person's faith and belief that nothing is impossible for Him.

She also was able to see the hand of God in everything. Shortly after a new lodge was completed in 1952, a Navy jet plane crashed into the mountain about 100 yards from the lodge. The pilot parachuted to safety, but about 20 acres of timber burned after the accident. Thankfully, the new lodge wasn't in the path of the fire.

"What a horrible thing!" said an observer.

"Thank God the lodge was spared!" said another.

Henrietta said, "Isn't it wonderful? We've been planning to build cabins on that very spot. Now the whole 20 acres is cleared and the plane that crashed has already dug the basement for the first cabin!"[4]

Today, Forest Home Ministries operates 7 distinct Christian camps in Southern California. The ministry offers 144 programs and welcomes some 40 denominations and more than 63,000 guests annually.

The ministry of faith, begun by Henrietta Mears, continues.

CHAPTER 7

Expendables

I have set the Lord always before me.

PSALM 16:8

How do you plan for a revival?

Start with impossibility.

See need. Throw in a climate ripe for change.

Then set it on fire.

* * *

"Impossible!" said the American ambassador in Rio de Janeiro. "Only official persons are allowed to have visas to Europe."

"But, I am official," said Henrietta quietly. "More than 700 young men from my church fought in Europe, and I want to see for myself what conditions prevail there, so that I can better counsel them as they return home."

The ambassador thought for a moment. "Let me make some calls," he said.

It was 1946. World War II had ended a year earlier. Germany was defeated. The atomic bomb had been dropped on Japan. Most of Europe was destroyed. There were heavy casualties on all sides. As the two dominant victors—America and Russia—sought to pick up the pieces, a new Cold War era of tension was ushered in.

The war years had taken their toll on Henrietta too. Faced with a scarcity of male leadership for her Sunday School, she had shouldered the increased responsibilities of ministering to servicemen, as well as the devastating task of comforting families that had lost sons. At the end of the war, Henrietta was exhausted and again experiencing extreme problems with her eyes.

She took a year's leave of absence from her responsibilities in Hollywood and traveled to South America with her sister, Margaret, to recoup her energies. They spent some extended time there on the calm beaches of Brazil. In all, the sisters would take 11 such trips over the years—three worldwide, the rest touching one or two continents. Some trips lasted for more than a year, some lasted for just a few months. During these trips, the sisters dedicated themselves to rest, renewal and education. Sometimes they visited missionaries and leaders who had been sent out from the church. Always, the change of pace provided relief from intensive ministry and gave Henrietta renewed perspective to return to her responsibilities. Henrietta was no armchair traveler! These were the days before the Internet. To best learn about the world, you had to go see it firsthand.

The ambassador did secure their visas to Europe, and Henrietta and Margaret sailed from South America. Henrietta spent most of her days on the ship resting, reading her Bible and praying, not realizing that God was preparing her for the most significant work of her life.

Henrietta's dining companion on the ship was a young French woman whose entire family had been killed during the war. When Henrietta and Margaret reached France, they wept as they saw the cities they had once known as majestic and proud—Rome, Brussels, Paris, Berlin—now broken and gray, overrun with crime and confusion. Children playing in the ruins occasionally triggered unexploded bombs; women lined up at relief kitchens seeking food for their families; soldiers limped back from war duty to homes of broken bricks and splintered beams; displaced people still searched for loved ones; and old folks sat silently, their eyes glazed over with the horrors and terrors of past days.

As she traveled from one devastated country to another, Henrietta recorded her impressions.

It's terrible to think of that which has come upon Europe! Nine people live in one room with no clothes but rags, no money, no food. Two out of three have tuberculosis. There are over five million orphans, bewildered and afraid. Their heads are often shaven as a precaution against lice. Christians have suffered indescribably for their faith. Their convictions have brought them persecution beyond those that men of lesser scruples endure.

Europe is on the brink of starvation. Last spring the floods and then the drought of summer resulted in scant harvests. Wheat and rye are 200 million bushels under last year, when hunger was widespread.

What is happening to our world?—crime, ruthlessness, killing, mass starvation, mass bombing, mass exportation of slaves! Germany is a vacuum; Nazism has left it with nothing. Hitler told the women that the highest service they could render was to sleep with German soldiers. Everything sacred was violated. Communism is reaching into the vacuum. Disillusionment and godlessness have taken over. Hardly anyone goes to church.

We are in an era of spiritual revolution. Men are rebelling against God.[1]

As Henrietta and Margaret boarded the boat for their return trip to America, Henrietta felt a growing awareness of God's leading; but she wanted to make sure, so she went to the Source of clarity and spent the return trip in meditation, prayer and Bible reading.

Henrietta's sense of God's calling her to do something did not go away once she was back in Hollywood. She felt as if she was being moved forward by an Unseen Hand. She had known His power in her life before, but this was a call beyond any previous experiences. Her speaking was filled with a new urgency. She spoke of what she had witnessed in Europe and what she believed was God's solution to the chaos. Those around her saw a new vitality and commitment that was even greater than before. She was living on the edge of expectancy; but what she was expecting was not yet clear. Henrietta and those around her began to pray that God would reveal what they were to do.

A Climate Ripe for Change

On Tuesday night, June 24, 1947, God broke through.

It was during the Gospel Light Teacher's Training Conference at Forest Home. Hundreds of Sunday School workers, pastors and young seminarians attended the conference. Henrietta told the group about the needs she had seen abroad. She asked the question, How was Hitler ever permitted to rise to power? The answer was that years earlier, the seeds of godlessness had been sown in that country and allowed to grow. She pointed to the growing concern of atheism (the doctrine that there is no God) as a prevalent worldview within communism. What happened in one godless society could happen just as easily in another. The world was not safe—not from political agendas or from the loss of true spirituality that could only be found in Jesus Christ. She spoke of the world's desperate need for godly leadership. Here are portions from her talk that evening.

Leaders are predicting that within another generation we will have entered World War III, which could bring an end to civilization.

God has an answer. Jesus said that we must make disciples of all men. We are to take His Gospel to the ends of the earth. We must become evangelists, even though evangelism is not recognized in our day as a valid program. And we must present the full doctrine of Christian truth.

God is looking for men and women of total commitment. During the war, men of special courage were called upon for difficult assignments; often those volunteers did not return. They were called "expendables." We must be expendables for Christ.[2]

Sitting in the audience that night were four young men who were powerfully moved by Henrietta's call to action: Louis Evans, Jr., the pastor's son and president of the college department at Hollywood First Presbyterian Church; Jack Franck, one of Henrietta's assistants in the Sunday School; Bill Bright, a young businessman who had just accepted Christ; and Rev. Richard Halverson, assistant pastor at the church. Richard was so discouraged in the ministry at the time that he was on the verge of quitting and returning to the pursuit of an acting career.

After Henrietta's talk, these four young men, along with several others, came to Henrietta's cabin for prayer and planning. As they knelt together, they were overcome by a sense of helplessness and inadequacy. They prayed all that night into the early hours of the next morning, crying out to the Lord, confessing sin, asking God for guidance, seeking the reality and power of the Holy Spirit.

And God answered—giving the men a vision. It was a specific call to action at a specific place—not a city or a people group, but an institution. The men saw the university campuses of the world filled with unsaved students who held in their hands the power to change the world. The university campuses held the key to world leadership and world revival.

Bill Bright wrote of the experience:

> It was a dramatic, marvelous experience. We knew the living God had come to take control. While we were all carried away with the sense of the holy presence of our God, our minds were racing with creative ideas.[3]

Out of their experience that night, the four men drafted a pledge to express on paper what they considered to be their responsibilities and to strategize and plan how to act on the enthusiasm God had given them. They based their pledge on the seal belonging to historic church leader John Calvin, which shows a hand offering a heart on fire. Around that was the inscription "My heart I give Thee, Lord, eagerly and sincerely."

They drafted a statement of commitment and listed four specific disciplines.

1. To pray, study the Bible and read devotional books not less than one hour per day.
2. To consistently live with Christ-like character.
3. To seek every opportunity to win the lost to Christ, and to witness at every opportunity.
4. To be completely sold-out for Christ in every area of life.[4]

They called their group the Fellowship of the Burning Heart.

That day—perhaps officially, perhaps unofficially—marked the beginning of what was to become a worldwide revival movement. The original leaders of the movement signed the pledge.

As word got out, others were invited to join the Fellowship.

Add Fire
The four young men went out into the early light of morning transformed, commissioned, expendable. Theirs was a world to reach for Christ, and the time was now!

A weekend college retreat at Forest Home that was already booked to happen two months later became the event to launch a movement. Under Henrietta's guidance, the four young men took it upon themselves to open the retreat to as many college students from as many campuses in the United States as possible. The length of the retreat was extended from a weekend to eight days. Additional speakers were contacted. Advertising was rushed across the country. The sheer audacity of what they contemplated—host a national collegiate conference with only two months to prepare—was amazing in a day when transportation and communication was nothing like it is today. Imagine having no Internet, no cell phones, no overnight mail delivery, and so on.

They changed the name of the conference to add the word "briefing"—Forest Home College Briefing Conference—to reflect the idea of how soldiers received their instructions before carrying out their missions. The goal of the conference was to prepare men and women to go out commissioned and trained to reach the world for Christ.

The conference was overtly evangelistic in a time when conferences themed around evangelism were unusual. At first, churches greeted the news of the conference with reserve, even coldness; but because of Henrietta's national reputation, they soon warmed up to the plan. Teams of collegians got busy and spread the news. The conference prep meetings were often characterized by intense times of worship, repentance and rededication of lives to the Lord and His work. Many trusted in Christ for their salvation for the first time, including—amazingly—one pastor.

One of the brochures that was sent out read:

A Call To Arms:

In the nineteenth century, God chose, through Dwight L. Moody, 60 Oxford University students as missionaries to carry the Gospel of Jesus Christ to the whole world.

In this twentieth century, He is calling for greater numbers. Youth from all walks of life, from our colleges and universities, from our businesses and industries, must go forth to carry this same Gospel to missions still in darkness.[5]

A notice taken around by deputation teams read in part:

God has spoken. The revival has started. On Tuesday night, June 24, at the Forest Home Christian Conference Grounds, the Holy Spirit spoke to a small group as they knelt in prayer in Miss Henrietta Mears's cabin. He gave them a vision with a plan for worldwide evangelism, filling them with the power of the Spirit in a manner not unlike the experience of the disciples at Pentecost. The Holy Spirit has continued to lead. Great and mighty things have been done since that unforgettable night a few short weeks ago.[6]

A personal letter sent out by Henrietta in regard to the conference contained this line:

I believe young men of today are going to do things that will stagger this generation.[7]

On opening day of the conference, college students arrived representing dozens of campuses from all over the country. Some arrived expectant and sincere; others were curious, skeptical, even cynical. In 1947, Forest Home could accommodate 500 guests. On the first day of the conference, 600 showed up, with many more continuing to pour in. Eventually, 87 college campuses from across America were represented. Those who came too late for a bed camped in cars or outside in the fields.

The speakers were well-known pastors and Christian leaders of the day, including Louis Evans, Sr., David Cowie and Robert Munger. The program was intentionally unscheduled. The leaders wanted the Holy Spirit to direct what would happen. Conference staff members spent hours in prayer leading up to and throughout the conference. The leaders spent the first afternoon in prayer as the students arrived.

The first meeting lasted for more than four hours, as did those on subsequent evenings. Student testimonies comprised the bulk of each meeting. Prayer, confession, forgiveness, cleansing, victory and the guidance of the Holy Spirit were central themes of each talk. Speakers talked about the need to be absolutely honest with God and to submit completely to His will. Students prayed that God's purpose for their lives would be fulfilled.

As the conference progressed, Henrietta posted a large map on a wall in the dining hall. She encouraged students to sign their names on the map at the location where they believed the Lord was calling them to serve. A student from USC wrote his name over Japan and went on to serve Christ there. Dick Halverson signed his name on China, and several years later he ministered there until God led him into other avenues of service. A recent seminary graduate, Christy Wilson, put his name on Afghanistan and went there.

For eight days, college students from across America breathed in the atmosphere of prayer, Scripture study and revival. When they returned to their college campuses, they took back what they had experienced. A spiritual movement was beginning to grow, nicknamed "the Expendables," started by the four young men who prayed for revival in Henrietta Mears's cabin.

At least four lasting results are believed to have come from this conference: The first was the beginning of a national revival among university students, with the effects still felt decades later. For instance, when Bill Bright spoke at college meetings well into the 1990s, he often encouraged groups to follow the same unscheduled format of relying on the Holy Spirit for guidance and direction during meetings.

The second result was the beginning of the annual College Briefing Conferences, which became a vehicle by which many young people entered vocational ministry over the next few years. The weeklong events soon ranked among the most important such events for the inspiration and training of university students in that era.

The third result was that two years later, in 1949, Billy Graham would experience a significant turning point in his walk of faith and ministry during a College Briefing Conference. Immediately after the conference, he conducted a crusade in Los Angeles that catapulted him into national prominence.

The fourth result was the formation of an outreach to actors and actresses, which came to be known as the Hollywood Christian Group. This group would go on to have a significant international influence for the cause of Christ.

Hollywood Christian Group

Attending the 1947 College Briefing Conference was a young Hollywood starlet named Colleen Townsend. Colleen was interested in spiritual things, but she wasn't a believer. She had attended the college group at Hollywood First Presbyterian for several months prior to the Conference along with her friend Louis Evans, Jr., one of the original members of the Fellowship of the Burning Heart group. At church, Colleen had heard the gospel presented several times, but she had never made a decision to give her life to Christ. On the Monday night of the Briefing Conference, Colleen prayed that Christ would show Himself to her. When she woke up the next morning, she had a calm assurance that she was saved.[8]

After her conversion, Colleen became actively involved in the college group at Hollywood First Presbyterian and grew in her faith. Henrietta had wondered how to reach people in the movie industry but had never been quite sure how to do it. Henrietta asked Colleen to help. Colleen phoned another actress, Connie Haines, who was a believer, and the two held the first meeting of the Hollywood Christian Group at Henrietta's house.

Creating a ministry to actors in Hollywood was a bold move. Movies and the theater were often considered taboo in Christian circles. Actors and actresses were sometimes considered to be of questionable character. As an acknowledged national Evangelical leader, Henrietta Mears demonstrated courage and love to help launch and mentor this group. Being famous could pose other challenges as well. For instance, actors Dennis Morgan and Virginia Mayo were Christians and attended Hollywood First Presbyterian, but often they had to deal with lingering stares from the curious. Miss Mayo frequently came on Sunday mornings with a hat covering most of her face. It would be difficult to create a ministry for this Hollywood actors' group based out of a church building, particularly if non-Christian personalities were to be reached.

The solution was to hold meetings in private homes, without publicity, the guests being brought by invitation only. The idea was to have a forum where Christian actors and actresses could invite their friends in the industry who were not Christians but were open to the gospel—a setting where famous people could come without being judged or exploited.

Some Christians didn't approve of the group, but that didn't stop Henrietta. Once, when Billy Graham was scheduled to be a guest speaker at one of the events, the meeting was to be held in actress Jane Russell's home. Miss Russell had played some film roles that some Christians didn't approve of. At that meeting, Henrietta put her arm around Jane Russell and said, "Isn't she darling?" Henrietta was a friend of show-business people. Not everyone was able to communicate the acceptance of Christ the way she did.

The Hollywood Group meetings proved spiritually successful. Tim Spencer, leader of the famous Cowboy singing group *The Sons of the Pioneers*, had been trapped by alcohol abuse for years. But he gave his life to Christ, was transformed and eventually became president of the Hollywood actors' group. Georgia Lee, a beautiful young dancer, with her husband, Ralph Hoopes, both became Christians as a result of coming to the group. Ralph eventually entered pastoral ministry. Actors Roy Rogers and Dale Evans became instrumental in the group, as did several other famous Hollywood industry people of that day.

As the group increased in size, it opened its doors to more people in the film industry than just the top stars, such as cameramen and technicians. Instead of meeting by invitation in homes, the meetings moved to the banquet hall of the Knickerbocker Hotel in Hollywood. In this way, what had started as an exclusive movement for a few took on a broader appeal. Other groups branched off from this central movement so that today several evangelistic efforts operate among the movie and television industry.

Launch Forward

The years 1947 and 1949, in particular, are considered high-water marks of revival. In succeeding years, Henrietta would look back on those earlier years as examples of what God can do if men and women are willing to fully commit themselves to Him. The first Briefing Conferences set the standard for collegians seeking the will of God.

The weeklong Briefings Conferences became one of the most important gatherings for the inspiration and training of university students of that era. In years to come, thousands of lives would be touched. Those lives would, in turn, begin other Christian organizations, lead people to Christ and influence many to give their lives to the ministry of following Jesus Christ and His purposes.

CHAPTER 8

Last Push Forward

Your strength will equal your days.

DEUTERONOMY 33:25

What is the connection between God's calling, hard work, endurance, difficulty and joy?

God's calling sometimes involves duty to go where life is difficult, sometimes for a season and sometimes for the rest of our lives. At other times, God's calling involves passion—we can't wait to get up each morning and see what the day holds. There are seasons during which we behave like Jonah or Moses when they were reluctant to follow God's voice. At other times we are a David or a Paul, eager to run with perseverance the race marked out for us. Regardless of our experiences, God's call always seems to be, as author Eugene Peterson has termed it, "a long obedience in the same direction."

Henrietta Mears's life appears to have been predominately one of passion: She seemed to thoroughly relish the position and place to which God had called her. Although little has been documented about Henrietta's struggles, she must have had some. She has been remembered for being hard-driving and perfectionistic. Surely that must have rubbed someone wrong once or twice. The schedule she kept is almost inhuman. Students remember her coming to a 6:00 A.M. Saturday prayer meeting, having already spent time alone with God in study and prayer.[1] Former president of Gospel Light, Bill Greig Jr., once commented that Henrietta made it a habit to be at work by 5:00 A.M. along with Ethel May Baldwin so that they could write Sunday School materials for three hours before working the regular day for the church.[2] Henrietta also worked late into the night, counseling students and attending functions. Others remember her spending up to 20 hours in Bible study and preparation for one 30-minute talk. Her personality could be relentless, and she was a tireless advocate for the work before her. In 1949, she was awarded an honorary Doctor of Humanities degree by Bob Jones University on the basis of her outstanding contributions to Christian education.

Henrietta Mears's life to the end was epitomized by victory. But it did not come easily. At least two trials marked Henrietta's latter years. These trials would shake her and cause her to rely even more steadfastly on the character of God, whom she had upheld and believed in for so many years.

Losing a Family Anchor

For more than 25 years, Henrietta lived with and relied on her older sister, Margaret. In many ways, Margaret made life and ministry possible for Henrietta. Margaret ran the household. She shopped, she cleaned, she entertained. She was a companion and peer. At the age of 72, Margaret was still quick-witted and individualistic. She could hold her own in discussions about politics, spirituality and trends with college students who came over to the house. She was described as the "down-to-earth" sister, who would sometimes dispense large doses of common sense when Henrietta's religious fervor (in Margaret's eyes) became impractical. Where Henrietta could keep people's hearts lifted and revved up, Margaret could keep people's feet on the ground.

Five days before Christmas 1951, as Margaret decorated the family home for the holidays, she suffered a stroke. Two days later, she passed away. College students, friends, family and church members mourned the passing of the woman they knew to be warm, funny, generous-hearted and devoted to the Lord.

The following Wednesday at a college prayer meeting, standing before 200 college students who knew her well, Henrietta described the dark water she was walking through surrounding her sister's death, and how the Lord was holding her up.

She said in part:

> I had thought that I would not come tonight. Then I realized what an opportunity I would be passing up if I did not come. I have been teaching you collegians for the last 25 years that God is able and that He does sustain us in any situation. I am here tonight to tell you that my God is able, and that He is my sufficiency at this very moment.
>
> As life passes you by, you will be going through experiences that you think you absolutely cannot endure. But God is faithful. He will not permit you to suffer a temptation that you will be incapable of bearing. And this I know, that if we will commit our way to Him, and will trust in Him, He will bring all these things to pass.[3]

When her sister died, Henrietta was faced with a pragmatic decision: What should she do about her large six-bedroom house? It seemed foolish for one woman to remain in something so large. But the thought of moving to a cramped apartment appalled her. And how could she ever have groups of students in an apartment?

As Henrietta weighed the pros and cons of where she should live, a good friend, knowing that Henrietta liked to tour beautiful homes, invited her to go and see a home across from the

UCLA campus. Located in Bel Air, the home was a virtual mansion with multiple rooms, sprawling grounds and large redwood trees outside. The home was actually larger than Henrietta's current home and presented many possibilities for ministry. In many ways, her ministry would go forward with the new house, not backward. For example, there was more space to host church functions and special interest groups, as well as provide lodging for traveling missionaries. Henrietta liked the home but needed to pray about the decision. If the home sold while she sought His will, then the Lord didn't want her to have it. When Henrietta learned that her dream house had been sold, it didn't faze her. After all, she had several speaking engagements coming up and a full roster of conferences booked at Forest Home.

The Lord didn't want her to have the house. The matter was settled.

A few days later she received a phone call that "something" had happened and another "For Sale" sign was on the house. Was she still interested?

Everything unfolded quickly. One of her former collegians was interested in buying her old house. Bill Bright, who was just beginning his new work with Campus Crusade for Christ based from the UCLA campus, along with his wife, Vonette, whom Henrietta had led to the Lord, offered to move into the new home with Henrietta to maintain the home and help her with expenses.

The Brights lived with Henrietta for the next 11 years. Vonette was the perfect hostess, taking over the household duties where Margaret had left off. In time, the Brights' first child, Zachary, was born, filling the home with liveliness. Beyond a shadow of a doubt, God had set His seal upon the entire venture.

One frequent visitor to their new house was a young UCLA football star named Donn Moomaw, who had come to know the Lord through Bill Bright's influence. Donn's new faith quickly caught fire; seeing the change in him, many others came to know Christ as well. When Donn finished university, he planned to go to seminary, intent on pursuing pastoral studies, but finances stood in his way. He had an offer to play professional football, but many of the games were held on Sunday, and his conscience was bothered by working on the Lord's Day. Donn committed his future to the Lord, rejected the professional football offer and applied to seminary. A short time later, another football contract was offered—this time with a league that didn't have Sunday play. Donn accepted and was able to secure his finances for school. He completed his studies and entered the ministry. In later years, Donn worked with Billy Graham for the Greater London Crusade.

The second challenge of Henrietta's latter years would come in 1951, shortly after returning from a trip around the world.

Henrietta had secured help to lead all her various responsibilities, but still the work had piled up. Most of it came in the form of counseling appointments—people seeking her counsel wanted to see her and no one else. When she came back from her trip, her counseling roster was booked solid. As usual, Henrietta jumped in full force. But she was now 61, and the constant exertion was taking its toll. Not long after returning to her ministry, Henrietta was speaking in front of a group of women from the church when she suddenly collapsed. She was rushed to the hospital where doctors revived her and performed multiple tests. Finding nothing, they offered no diagnosis, only the recommendation to take things easier.

Other physical problems began for Henrietta in the years that followed. Once, as she recuperated in the hospital, Ethel May told her, "This is the Lord's way of letting you get away from everyone's problems."

In 1957, while sailing with friends across the Pacific, Henrietta realized that her eyesight was once again deteriorating. Even more ominous, pains in her eyes were rapidly increasing. The sight in her better eye also became impaired. After arriving in Australia, the new trouble was diagnosed as a ruptured blood vessel. Medical authorities advised Henrietta to return to the States to see her doctor there. When Henrietta returned to California, her eye doctor examined her and said there was nothing he could do for her condition. He advised her to pray.

Henrietta knew that her sight lay in the hands of God, who had created it, and that God alone could intervene and stop the deterioration from taking place. She prayed, and asked many others to pray with her. The next time the doctor examined her eyes, the deterioration had stopped in her good eye.

Practically, Henrietta responded to these physical challenges by shifting some responsibilities to other people. For instance, as the influence of Gospel Light Publications grew beyond expectations, Henrietta shifted the leadership of the organization to Dr. Cyrus Nelson. Dr. Nelson was one of Henrietta's former collegians and had also been profoundly influenced at Forest Home.

At the same time, Henrietta continued forward with the vision of seeing others come to know the Lord. Her world travels had left her restless to branch out even further. A new ministry was about to be birthed.

One Last Push

The seeds for this new ministry were first sown in 1952, just after Margaret's death, and after Henrietta had recuperated from her first physical collapse.

Henrietta and Esther Ellinghusen, the schoolteacher who wrote curriculum for Gospel Light when it first began, decided to take a trip around the world, concentrating on visiting schools, mission stations and hospitals. One evening in Hong Kong, some missionaries drove them through the red-light district of the city and invited the two Americans to help pass out tracts to the prostitutes. Colorful and creative tracts were considered cutting-edge material in the 1950s, and there on the street, Henrietta and Esther handed out hundreds of gospel brochures and leaflets. Later, on university campuses in Japan, they saw students reading well-printed communist literature while Christian material was either scant or nonexistent. On that same trip, the two visited with many missionaries who all said the same thing: Getting quality Christian literature and Sunday School material—particularly in languages other than English—was a huge problem.

On the return trip, the two women began to process all they had experienced. The enormous need for Christian literature in other languages burdened Henrietta's and Esther's hearts.

Although she didn't know it at the time, Henrietta had already influenced initial efforts at producing gospel literature in other languages. One of her female college students had gone to Guatemala and had started a translation program there. She had found the job an immense one, however, and after much work and prayer, found a man with printing knowledge who could read, proof and lay out the pages of the material. Word also came of a missionary in Japan who had quite a bit of experience translating Gospel Light's Sunday School lessons. He and his wife previously had been missionaries in Peking (now Beijing), China, and had translated and printed materials there. When Peking became a troubled area, he moved the work to Shanghai. Eventually, China was closed and the couple had to evacuate, leaving behind the Gospel Light materials they had translated and printed there. Undaunted, the couple went to Japan, learned that language and again began a translation program.

This information encouraged Henrietta and Gospel Light. In many ways, the work had already begun. Reports and letters had come in steadily from various parts of the world asking for Sunday School literature in other languages. What would Henrietta do to meet this ever-growing need?

In 1961, when Henrietta was 71, she called together the various leaders in Gospel Light to found a new organization—Gospel Literature in National Tongues—later changed to Gospel Literature International—GLINT for short. From the start, the company's aim was to produce quality curriculum for distribution internationally. With the same passion with which she had provided curriculum in Hollywood, Henrietta wanted to put the best possible Bible-teaching tools in the hands of teachers and learners around the world. GLINT was a separate organization from Gospel Light, but Gospel Light allowed GLINT to use its materials for free, adapting and translating them for publication in foreign languages.

From the beginning, Cy Nelson, the president of Gospel Light, had a special love for the ministry of GLINT. He volunteered to assist the newly established foundation in a dual capacity: He served as the first chairman of its board of directors; and since the organization initially had no paid staff, he acknowledged gifts to the organization and handled other paperwork necessary to the ministry's operations until the first executive director took over for him.

When GLINT's Board made known the needs of various projects to interested friends, the first funds came in for translation programs in India, South and Central America and Europe. The vision caught fire as missionaries pledged their support and time to get the materials out, and money was raised. Within a short period, more than 100,000 children were reading Gospel Light Sunday School books in Greece. Translations of the same books were being introduced into major linguistic areas of India under the supervision of another missionary.

Stories began to pour in about how God was using this new organization. In India, a young man had lost his fingers to leprosy and couldn't work, but he was skilled in languages, although he couldn't hold a pen to write. He had recently converted to Christianity from Hinduism. He found a friend who could act as his scribe. Together they worked on translation projects.

There were reports of churches in other countries doubling and tripling in a few months' time as new Sunday School manuals were produced. As had happened in Hollywood, now in dozens of other places in Asia, Africa and elsewhere, young people were being introduced to the gospel of Jesus Christ. This important work continues through the ministry called Gospel Light Worldwide.

Today Gospel Light Worldwide (GLW) continues to provide culturally relevant Bible curriculum for children, youth and families, as well as books and resources for adults through strategic partnerships with indigenous publishers, ministries and organizations. GLW partners with more than 200 publishers in 50 different languages.

For as Long as Possible

In Henrietta's latter years, she sometimes pondered the question of retirement. But if she retired, what would she do then? Whenever she thought about retiring, the answer always came back the same: Don't. Whenever she took steps in that direction, some new challenge would develop and she would rise to meet it. Late in life she resolved that retirement was out of the question for her. She might slow down a bit, but not much. She wanted to serve and remain as active as she could for as long as possible.

Into her late 60s and early 70s she continued to open her home to guests seeking spiritual guidance. She was present at most of the functions of the college department, teaching, counseling and training leaders. The executives of the college class continued to meet with her on Saturday mornings, although sometimes her health held her back. Sometimes it seemed to them as if Henrietta was seeing if God's specific promise to Old Testament saints applied to her as well: "Your strength will equal your days" (Deut. 33:25).

In her final years, she continued to seek, stretch and search untapped reservoirs of God's love, always wanting to know Christ more fully and make Him more fully known. She studied the Word to rely upon the Holy Spirit even more. Friends say that the fruits of the Spirit became even more evident in Henrietta's life the older she became. Her life was marked by a new sense of holiness and peace, and she became more sympathetic, gracious, kind and secure.

Her eyes were just beginning to glimpse the opening doors of eternity, and she wanted to stay strong with Christ until the end.

CHAPTER 9

Homegoing

I have fought the good fight, I have finished the race, I have kept the faith.

2 TIMOTHY 4:7

How do you mark the success of a life? Henrietta Mears would never say success was about numbers. The goal was always about changed hearts. Whose hearts—and *how many* hearts—was up to the Holy Spirit.

Perhaps like the parable of the talents, a life can be measured by faithfulness in using the gifts you've been given—starting strong wherever you're at, persevering in the race no matter what challenges or setbacks you encounter and, unlike King Solomon who started well but finished poorly, arriving at the end of your life still walking wholeheartedly, steadfastly, resolutely and unswervingly with the Lord.

A Song for Next Year

Early in 1963, Henrietta attended a garden party sponsored by some of the women of the church. When she saw a musical friend in the crowd, Henrietta asked her to play something for them on the piano.

"Oh, Miss Mears," said the woman, "I'm really not in practice. I'll play something for you next year."

Henrietta registered a kindly disappointment. Only a friend standing next to her heard the whisper "I'll not be here next year."[1]

During the day of Monday, March 18, 1963, Ethel May Baldwin took Henrietta, now 73, for a ride in her car. The women drove past construction sites in the San Fernando Valley. They talked with excitement about the rapid expansion of Southern California, of the influx of people to the area and of the opportunities they would have to reach these new residents with the gospel of Jesus Christ. When Ethel May drove Henrietta back to her home in Bel Air, both women were still talking animatedly about what the future would bring.

Tuesday, Henrietta did not leave the house. That evening she talked at length on the phone with the director of Forest Home, Jack Franck, about the coming prospects at the conference center—so many new ideas were in the offing. Henrietta, a visionary as always, was planning for the future.

She went to bed that night with partially prepared study notes laying on her desk for an upcoming series for the college group, including a message she had planned for her collegians at their Easter breakfast.

The next morning, her housekeeper found her. Henrietta Mears had died peacefully in her sleep, slipping through the veil between the present and eternity, the veil she had described over the years as being so very thin.

*   *   *

Nearly 2,000 people filed into the sanctuary of the Hollywood First Presbyterian Church to witness one of the most triumphant memorial services they would ever see. Scattered throughout the audience that day were hundreds of people whom Henrietta Mears had personally led to Christ.

The opening words of the service were from John 11:25-26: "I am the resurrection and the life: he that believeth in me, though he were dead, yet shall he live: and whosoever liveth and believeth in me shall never die." A soloist, one of Henrietta's collegians, sang the classic hymn "How Great Thou Art." The church choir sang Martin Luther's majestic hymn "A Mighty Fortress Is Our God."

Many tributes to Henrietta Mears were spoken, including one sent by telegram from Billy Graham, which read in part, "I am certain that Henrietta Mears had a great reception in heaven. She made a tremendous impact upon my life and ministry." One pastor spoke of Henrietta's energy, enthusiasm and ability to challenge people to live the lives God intended for them. Another mentioned her talent for showing a person his or her unlimited capacity to be filled with God's ability. Dr. Richard Halverson, who went on to be chaplain of the U.S. Senate, recalled her wise counsel, especially concerning her advice to stay in one place in order to establish a lasting work and not move about from church to church. Henrietta's work at Hollywood First Presbyterian Church was possible, said Halverson, because she stayed there for 35 years, turning down many invitations to minister elsewhere.

Rev. Louis Evans, Jr. gave a fitting tribute through a prayer:

O Lord, we look upon heaven now and can see nothing but rejoicing, for she is meeting all those whom she has known on this earth who have gone before and all those whom she has not known on this earth who have waited for her all these years. Indeed, O Lord, heaven throbs with rejoicing on this day for thy saint, who walked in simple victory, because she walked in simple trust.[2]

In his tribute, Dr. Cyrus Nelson summarized the many accomplishments of Henrietta Mears:

> Because of Dr. Mears's deep love of her Savior and her church, she had a great love for the world. She believed that for the needs of all people in all places, Christ was the answer. Consequently, when she envisaged the world of the local church, she saw the Church universal.
>
> "People must be called by God," she said, and she prayed the Lord of the harvest to send forth His laborers. It is a remarkable fact that over 400 young people went into Christian service under her influence. [Last year] in 1962, there were more than 40,000 delegates at Forest Home, coming from 40 different denominations and hundreds of churches and groups.
>
> Billy Graham, in 1949, found a renewed dedication at Forest Home, which enabled him to begin his now-famous Los Angeles Crusade. Dr. Mears also played an important part in the worldwide ministry of Campus Crusade for Christ. Bill Bright, the founder, listened to her one evening with intensity and conviction and, after her challenge, he knelt before God. This was his spiritual pivot from self to Savior.
>
> Then Henrietta Mears opened up the doors of her home and, for almost 10 years, thousands of students crossed Sunset Boulevard from UCLA to hear the gospel there. The Hollywood Christian Group was born in her home. She was a founder of the National Sunday School Association, and a member of many boards of international Christian significance.
>
> Her global vision also saw the potential of the printing press, and in 1933 she founded Gospel Light Publications,

together with Esther Ellinghusen, Ethel May Baldwin and Stanley Engle. Today this ministry touches more than 20,000 churches and mission stations across our country and overseas.

Her last worldwide ministry is GLINT, a missionary foundation formed to translate and distribute Christian materials around the world. GLINT was born in 1961.[3]

Henrietta Mears's open casket was banked with flowers. Her memorial service was concluded with Handel's "Hallelujah Chorus" from *The Messiah,* and the congregation rose to honor God and pay tribute to Henrietta Mears—leader, mentor and friend.

She was buried at Forest Lawn Memorial Park in Los Angeles. Officials there said that the crowd attending the graveside service was the largest gathered in 20 years—an astounding fact, considering that many of Hollywood's greats are also buried there. She left her estate to the ministry of Forest Home, the conference center she founded 25 years earlier.

How Immense the Circle

When Henrietta Mears was a young woman, she wrote a pamphlet that outlined her dedication as a teacher. In many ways, this description both served as a guide and a report card for her life. In part, the pamphlet spoke of the following goals:

- She aimed to win everybody she met to Christ.
- When someone she knew made a decision for Christ, she aimed to help establish him or her in daily Bible reading and prayer, as well as "to put helpful books in [the person's] hands," and to show him or her the importance of church work and uniting with God's people. She

would stay accessible to this person and see that he or she found a specific place to serve.

- Christianity is about salvation, but it is also about being the hands and feet of Christ. Henrietta aimed to bring Christianity to everyday life by feeding the hungry, helping the poor, and more.

- She aimed to help each person she met recognize his or her talents and then use those talents for God's glory. She hoped to instill in each person a divine discontent for the pettiness of life, as well as giving each person a vision of great things that can be done enthusiastically and passionately for the Lord.

- She resolved to make herself accessible to anyone who wanted to talk about deep matters, and to never express disappointment with anyone.

- She aimed to pray continually for wisdom and power.

- She resolved to not seek rest nor ease, but to run with perseverance the race marked out for her. In this race, she resolved not to fail Christ.[4]

Did she live up to her goals?

Henrietta Mears was involved in virtually the whole range of Christian ministries—church work, camping, conferences, publications, missions, small groups, discipleship, speaking, teaching, leadership training, and more. Each of these areas were freshened and changed as a result of her influence. Her legacy endures through contemporary approaches to Bible study and Sunday School material, the ministries she founded and the lives of outstanding Christian leaders who have impacted the world for Christ.

It is amazing to think that Henrietta Mears was not necessarily young when she began the career that was to become her life work and that would have such an impact for generations to come. She stayed in that job for 35 years, and from that one platform at Hollywood First Presbyterian Church she would get involved in a wide arena of ministries that impacted not only her immediate sphere of influence, but also influenced the world for Christ.

Henrietta Mears had perhaps the most far-reaching spiritual impact of any woman of the twentieth century. The scope of her work extended worldwide and her influence continues today, generations after her passing. *Christianity Today* magazine dubbed her "the grandmother of us all,"[5] because her vision of the Christian life so greatly inspired the young people of her day who in turn passed this vision on to contemporary Christians.

In 1959, at a teacher training conference at Forest Home, Henrietta offered what could well be considered her epitaph. These are her words:

When I get old and decrepit, I'm going to draw myself up to a television and hear my voice speak around the world. It's just wonderful to think that what we speak and do are translated some way, in a most mystical and marvelous way, to other individuals and they in turn spread it out and out and out until the circle is so immense that we haven't any idea.

Men and women, if you had been teaching in a Sunday School then left that church and in 10 years went back to the same place only to find one young man who rushes up to you and grips you by the arm and says: "It was in your class that I found Christ," you know, there would be a lump in your throat. And what would you say? Well, I thank God that there is one person I absolutely touched for God! You don't have to be great. But you can pass on to another the Lord Jesus Christ and He, in turn, will make that man or woman whom He wishes them to be.

What has God told you to do today? Would you go home and write down some decision? Don't write down ten decisions. Write down one decision that you'll do. And ask God to give you courage to fulfill that decision.[6]

How immense the circle of a life lived well.

CHAPTER 10

Postscript

You may have read the story of Henrietta Mears's life and felt challenged and inspired—and even a bit conflicted. *That's nice for her,* you might think, *but that certainly could never be me. Henrietta Mears is superhuman, a type of early generation Wonder Woman. Whatever she touched turned to spiritual gold.*

It's important to note that this is indeed her story, and not ours. God endowed Henrietta Mears with a specific set of skills to use for a specific place and time. We are not her; but neither are we asked to be her. God is writing our own stories right now, and those stories are as detailed and exclusive as the most unique of all His creations.

There are certain insights, however, that we can take away from the story of Henrietta Mears. These patterns are helpful as a guide to become all that God intends for us to be. Consider, then, a few applications from an unusual life that we can apply to our own.

*   *   *

Henrietta Mears lived a life outside the box, whatever box there was. In 1927, for a single woman to take risks, cast vision, head organizations, even to lead men, was unusual. It's true that Hollywood offered her an unusually accepting climate, open to innovation; but her innovations were atypical for the day and age, particularly in faith-based environments that can be prone to resisting change and originality.

What are the boxes of our lives? These boxes inherently may not be wrong, yet they may confine us to preconceived notions of what life should be.

- Are you a young mother who wants to go to seminary? Step out of the box.
- Are you a business professional who longs to minister overseas? Step out of the box.
- Are there any cultural expectations that are trapping you to *not* follow God's calling in your life? Step out of the box, break the mold and follow Christ.

Henrietta Mears reached a balance between accepting the limitations of her life while neither ignoring nor downplaying her strengths. We never read of Henrietta bemoaning what she didn't have. Rather, we read of her optimism and betterment with what she did have. What were her limitations? Poor eyesight, parents who died when she was young and, perhaps, her lack of a husband in a Christian culture that tends to mistrust singleness. No matter. She turned her poor eyesight into a tool to develop exemplary study patterns. Her lack of a family of origin enabled her to move cross county more easily. Her singleness became the catalyst to forge intimate relationships with a wide spectrum of people from all ages and backgrounds.

And what of her strengths? Henrietta Mears grew up in a world of privilege and responsibility. She received and internalized a legacy of expecting to help others and to better the world around her. And she saw what she had been given as a plus. Similarly, her earlier career as a schoolteacher developed in her the skills of public speaking, the ability to organize on a large scale and the ability to artfully and professionally lead people by the principles she taught. When the job at Hollywood First Presbyterian Church opened, she already had the necessary ingredients to be successful there. Yet she didn't become stagnant. Her life was continually characterized by study, diligence and a commitment to her craft.

What are your strengths and limitations? Are you stymied by your frailties? Or at the other end of the spectrum, are you overwhelmed with too much potential? If we could hear Henrietta today, she would say to us, "Wherever you are, start where you are. Depend on the Holy Spirit to help you moved forward; then move. Use your initiative to work hard and work well—use whatever you've been through and whatever you've been given."

Henrietta Mears committed her life wholeheartedly to Christ. Perhaps this insight is her most important legacy. She was relentless in her goal *to know Christ and to make Him known.* From that path there would be no swerving.

Surely there must have been temptations for her: opportunities for laziness, lust, greed—any of the wrong choices that are continually offered to all of us. But hers was a life lived in the light of God's grace and unreservedly, unconditionally, sold out to Christ. The disciplines of her life did not make her holy; only Christ could do that. But those disciplines allowed her the freedom to live a life worth emulating.

A similar life can be ours. Henrietta wrote:

> Isn't it strange how evil lurks in success as well as in failure, in health and in sickness, in companionship and in loneliness? One hour's association with a person who is not good may leave in the soul a suggestion of evil that will work utter ruin in a man's life. Determine so to live in Christ that by your life you will compel man to think

of Christ; God's wisdom to know His will; God's power to do His will—this is really living.[1]

And what about you? You are not called to be Henrietta Mears; you are called to live your life, your story. Will you commit today to the will of Jesus Christ, to live the amazing life He beckons you to lead?

Dr. Henrietta C. Mears
1890-1963

Born in Fargo, North Dakota,	October 23, 1890
Conversion, baptism, First Baptist Church of Minneapolis	Easter Sunday, 1897, age 7
Taught first Sunday School class, First Baptist Church	1901, age 11
Made commitment to vocational Christian service, at first believing her call was to be a missionary to China	1907, age 17
Graduated from the University of Minnesota	1913, age 23
Schoolteacher, public school system, Minneapolis	1913-1928, age 23-38
Director of Christian Education and Teacher of College Department, First Presbyterian Church of Hollywood	1928-1963, age 38-73
Founder, Gospel Light Publications	1933, age 43
Founder, Forest Home Christian Conference Center	1938, age 48

Honored with Doctor of Humanities degree   1949, age 49

Founder, GLINT   1960, age 70

Died at home in Bel Air, California   March 20, 1963, age 73

Endnotes

Introduction

1. Michael Richardson, *Amazing Faith, the Authorized Biography of Bill Bright* (Colorado Springs, CO: Waterbrook, 2000), adapted pp. 19-44.
2. Billy Graham, *Just As I Am* (San Francisco: HarperCollins, 1997), adapted pp. 143-158.
3. Barbara Hudson, *The Henrietta Mears Story* (Grand Rapids, MI: Revell, 1957), p. 99.

Chapter 1

1. Anna Kerr, personal interview by Andrea Madden, tape-recorded Hollywood, CA, October 1996, *Henrietta Mears: 1890-1963, Her Life and Influence*, unpublished master's thesis, Gordon-Conwell Theological Seminary, 1997, p. 1.
2. Betsy Cox, *Henrietta Mears as a Christian Educator*, unpublished master's thesis, Fuller Theological Seminary, 1961, pp. 50-51.
3. Michael Richardson, *Amazing Faith, the Authorized Biography of Bill Bright* (Colorado Springs, CO: Waterbrook, 2000), pp. 21-22.
4. Eleanor Doan, *431 Quotes from the Notes of Henrietta Mears* (Glendale, CA: Regal, 1970), p. 38.
5. Barbara Hudson, *The Henrietta Mears Story* (Grand Rapids, MI: Revell, 1957), p. 51.
6. Henrietta Mears, *The Romance of the Sunday School* and *Who Are the Young People You Teach?* Transcriptions of talks quoted as appendixes in Ethel May Baldwin and David Benson, *Henrietta Mears and How She Did It* (Ventura, CA: Regal, 1966), pp. 291, 311.
7. Doan, *431 Quotes*, p. 43.
8. Earl Roe, *Dream Big, the Henrietta Mears Story* (Ventura, CA: Regal, 1990), p. 98.

Chapter 2

1. Ethel May Baldwin and David Benson, *Henrietta Mears and How She Did It* (Ventura, CA: Regal, 1966), p. 305.
2. Eleanor Doan, *431 Quotes from the Notes of Henrietta Mears* (Glendale, CA: Regal, 1970), p. 73.
3. Baldwin and Benson, *Henrietta Mears and How She Did It*, pp. 335-336.

4. Ibid., p. 293.

5. Barbara Hudson, *The Henrietta Mears Story* (Grand Rapids, MI: Revell, 1957), p. 101.

6. Ibid., pp.106-107.

7. Earl Roe, *Dream Big, the Henrietta Mears Story* (Ventura, CA: Regal, 1990), p. 74.

8. Hudson, *The Henrietta Mears Story,* p. 112.

Chapter 3

1. Barbara Hudson, *The Henrietta Mears Story* (Grand Rapids, MI: Revell, 1957), p. 166.

2. Ibid., pp.119-120.

3. Ibid., p. 120.

4. Earl Roe, *Dream Big, the Henrietta Mears Story* (Ventura, CA: Regal, 1990), p. 81.

5. Ibid., p. 82.

6. Hudson, *The Henrietta Mears Story,* p. 125.

Chapter 4

1. Earl Roe, *Dream Big, the Henrietta Mears Story* (Ventura, CA: Regal, 1990), p. 92.

2. Barbara Hudson, *The Henrietta Mears Story* (Grand Rapids, MI: Revell, 1957), pp. 62-65.

3. Ibid., pp. 63-64.

4. Ibid., pp. 64-65.

5. Ethel May Baldwin and David Benson, *Henrietta Mears and How She Did It* (Ventura, CA: Regal, 1966), pp. 292-295. (The illustration of Knott's Berry Farm was given by Henrietta Mears at a Baptist General Conference convention, Portland, Oregon, 1957.)

Chapter 5

1. Ethel May Baldwin and David Benson, *Henrietta Mears and How She Did It* (Ventura, CA: Regal, 1966), p. 298.

2. Barbara Hudson, *The Henrietta Mears Story* (Grand Rapids, MI: Revell, 1957), p. 148.

3. Earl Roe, *Dream Big, the Henrietta Mears Story* (Ventura, CA: Regal, 1990), p. 149.

Chapter 6

1. Earl Roe, *Dream Big, the Henrietta Mears Story* (Ventura, CA: Regal, 1990), p. 237.

2. Ethel May Baldwin and David Benson, *Henrietta Mears and How She Did It* (Ventura, CA: Regal, 1966), pp. 192-194.

3. John Fawcett (1740-1817), "Blest Be the Tie That Binds," public domain.
4. Barbara Hudson, *The Henrietta Mears Story* (Grand Rapids, MI: Revell, 1957), p. 180.

Chapter 7
1. Earl Roe, *Dream Big, the Henrietta Mears Story* (Ventura, CA: Regal, 1990), pp. 275-277.
2. Ibid., pp. 279-280.
3. Michael Richardson, *Amazing Faith, the Authorized Biography of Bill Bright* (Colorado Springs, CO: Waterbrook, 2000), pp. 36-37.
4. Ibid., pp. 37-38.
5. Roe, *Dream Big, the Henrietta Mears Story,* p. 285.
6. Ibid., p. 286.
7. Ibid., p. 288.
8. Andrea Madden, *Henrietta C Mears 1890-1963, Her Life and Influence*, unpublished master's thesis, Gordon-Conwell Theological Seminary (South Hamilton, MA: 1997), p. 103.

Chapter 8
1. Andrea Madden, *Henrietta C Mears 1890-1963, Her Life and Influence*, unpublished master's thesis, Gordon-Conwell Theological Seminary (South Hamilton, MA: 1997), p. 115.
2. Ibid., p. 116.
3. Ethel May Baldwin and David Benson, *Henrietta Mears and How She Did It* (Ventura, CA: Regal, 1966), p. 261.

Chapter 9
1. Ethel May Baldwin and David Benson, *Henrietta Mears and How She Did It* (Ventura, CA: Regal, 1966), p. 277.
2. Earl Roe, *Dream Big, the Henrietta Mears Story* (Ventura, CA: Regal, 1990), p. 335.
3. Ibid., pp. 336-337.
4. Henrietta Mears, *The Dedication of a Teacher*, Gospel Light Archives.
5. W. M. Zoba, "The Grandmother of Us All," *Christianity Today*, 40 (10) September 16, 1996, pp. 44-46.
6. Henrietta Mears, *How to Become a Great Sunday School Teacher*, unpublished transcript of speech given at Forest Home, 1959. Gospel Light archives.

Postscript
1. Eleanor Doan, *431 Quotes from the Notes of Henrietta Mears* (Glendale, CA: Regal, 1970), pp. 94, 96.

Get the Best-Selling Books About the Best-Seller Ever

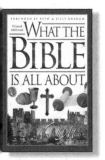

What the Bible Is All About Bible Handbook Visual Edition
Foreword by Billy Graham
NIV Text with over 500 Full-Color Photographs and Illustrations
Henrietta Mears
Hardcover
ISBN 08307.43294

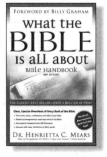

What the Bible Is All About Bible Handbook KJV Edition
Over 4 Million in Print
Henrietta Mears
Paperback
ISBN 08307.30869

What the Bible Is All About Bible Handbook NIV Edition
The Classic Best-Seller with over 4 Million in Print
Henrietta Mears
Paperback
ISBN 08307.30850

What the Bible Is All About Bible Handbook Reference Library CD-ROM
Everything You Want to Know About the Bible—FAST!
Henrietta Mears
UPC 607135.003984

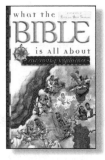

What the Bible Is All About Bible Handbook for Young Explorers
Foreword by Ruth and Billy Graham
Frances Blankenbaker
Paperback • ISBN 08307.23633

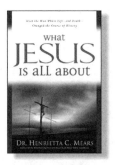

What Jesus is All About
Meet the Man Whose Life—and Death—Changed the Course of History
Henrietta Mears
ISBN 08307.33272

Available at Bookstores Everywhere!
Visit **www.regalbooks.com** to join **Regal's FREE e-newsletter.**
You'll get useful **excerpts from our newest releases** and **special access to online chats with your favorite authors.** Sign up today!

Regal
God's Word for Your World™
www.regalbooks.com